Fun on the run

324 INSTANT F·A·M·I·L·Y ACTIVITIES

Fun on the run

324
INSTANT
F·A·M·I·L·Y
ACTIVITIES

By Cynthia L. Copeland

Illustrated by Sanford Hoffman

Workman Publishing, New York

Library of Congress Cataloging-in-Publication Data is available
ISBN 0-7611-3448-4

Design by Paul Hanson

Workman books are available at special discount
when purchased in bulk for premiums and sales promotions
as well as for fund-raising or educational use.
Special editions or book excerpts also can be created to
specification. For details, contact the Special Sales Director
at the address below.

Workman Publishing Company, Inc.
708 Broadway
New York, NY 10003-9555
www.workman.com

Printed in the United States of America

First printing June 2004
10 9 8 7 6 5 4 3

We do not remember days . . .
we remember moments.

—Cesare Pavese

For Anya, Alex, Aaron,
Andrew, and Brad,
who know how to have fun
on the run.

Acknowledgments

Many thanks to my editor, Margot
Herrera, for her great suggestions
and support. Thanks also to Paul
Hanson and Elizabeth Johnsboen,
who did the wonderful design
work. As always, I couldn't have
written this without my helpful
friends at the Keene Public Library.

Contents

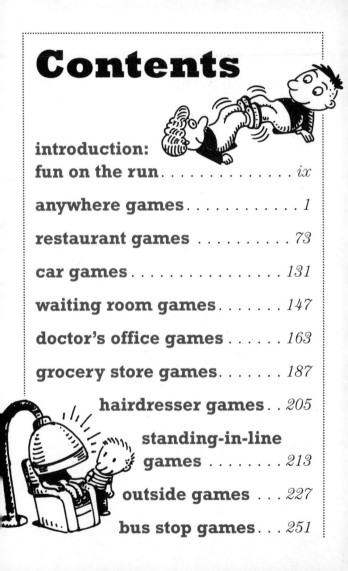

contents

introduction

Doesn't it seem that you and your kids spend half your time together on the go and the other half waiting? We rush to make it to a doctor's appointment, then wait 45 minutes to be seen. We dash to soccer practice (and make it with two minutes to spare!), but then wait with a fussy toddler for practice to end. We hurry to the bank to slip in before closing time, then stand in line and try to convince our three-year-old not to scribble on all of the deposit slips.

These odd pockets of waiting time— which seem like a virtual breeding ground for temper tantrums and whiny exchanges—can actually be opportunities for fun (and even educational!) games. No matter where you and your kids are, there's a way to make fun. Make fun in the grocery store by playing the Toilet Paper Toss. Make fun in the pediatrician's office by blowing up a disposable glove and playing Keep Away. Make fun in line at the bank with Trash Can Ball.

Teaching our kids to take pleasure in the most mundane everyday activities is one of the best gifts we can give them. After all, they'll take many more trips to the post office and to the laundromat than they will to Disneyland.

It's not as hard to engage kids in games as you might think, because kids approach life looking for fun. So if we act like the grocery store is an exciting place to visit, they'll happily buy into that. A parent's enthusiasm is contagious.

This book is full of great ideas for ways parents can entertain their children (from toddlers to teens) during what is called in-between time—no props needed. Some games require parental supervision or participation; others are meant for children to play on their own. Many of the games can be played anywhere, whether you're in a line

or in the car. But some activities
are better suited to certain places
than to others, so there are sections
for specific locations—restaurants,
the doctor's office, the grocery
store, the bus stop, even the hairdresser, to name a few. Most of the
games are great for kids of varying
ages to play, though some require
more sophisticated reading and
reasoning skills. Babies and toddlers
have their very own chapter at the
end of the book. And after that
you'll find
short pieces
on topics like
how to quash
bickering and sug-
gestions for making
snack time fun.

It does take some extra
effort to turn a visit
to the dry cleaner
into a fun adventure.
But just remember,
as a parent you
never know when you're making
a memory. You may think that
the kids will always remember the
giraffes at the San Diego Zoo, but it's
a lot more likely they'll remember
the Raindrop Race game you
played in the car on the way there.
So turn to page 143 and teach
them how to play!

anywhere games

The title of this category speaks for itself; these games can be played anywhere. Use them to supplement another category or refer to them if you find yourself waiting with your child somewhere not specifically mentioned in this book. No special items—menus, paper cups, magazines—are needed (though some games call for coins, pens, or other items likely to be in your purse). Just add kids for instant fun!

Secret Word

Take turns choosing a secret word (it can be anything: *pickles, cupcake, ponytail, hair* . . .). Begin talking, substituting the word *goober* for your secret word. How long will you have to talk about the *goober* before the others figure out what it is?

Sounds Like . . .

A child can imitate a noise while the others guess. He can try sounding like running water, a vacuum, wind, rain, running feet, or a train. Who makes the best sound effects?

A variation: Everyone closes his or her eyes but one person. She makes a noise (clinks coins together, turns an object over, pushes back her chair . . .), and whoever guesses how she made the noise becomes the next noisemaker!

Clap, Tap, and Snap

One person begins this game by making a sound or action pattern (like three claps). The next person repeats it, then adds another (three claps, then two finger snaps). The third player repeats the actions of the first two players, then adds his own—maybe foot stamps, air kisses, or ear tugs. The game continues with each player repeating what the previous person did and then adding actions of his own until someone makes a mistake. Then the game begins again!

5 Mind-Benders

Ask your kids these riddles:

1. Forward I am heavy but backward I am not. What am I?

2. The more you have of it, the less you can see. What is it?

3. What is in the middle of nowhere?

4. What gets whiter the dirtier it gets?

5. What is better than the best, more evil than demons, the poor have it and the rich need it, and if you eat it, you will die?

ANSWERS: The word *ton;* 2. Darkness; 3. The letter *h;* 4. A chalkboard; 5. Nothing

Bag of Mystery

No matter where you are, you always have your purse! Your children can take turns guessing what is inside. Ask, "Do you think there is a comb in my purse?" or "Do you think there is a penny in my purse?" You can award points for correct guesses and give away something from your purse (a mint or a dime) to the one who receives the most points. (A dad can ask wallet questions, but he will have to be a little shrewder to make the game interesting: "Do I have a picture of a president in my wallet?")

Hand Puppets

Remember this one from decades past? Have your child make a fist with her thumb positioned on the side of the fingers rather than tucked underneath them. Now draw two eyes on the side of her index finger's knuckle and draw lips around the opening created by the placement of her thumb. She can move her thumb and "talk" to her siblings (or she can use her hand puppet to ask the receptionist or server how much longer the wait will be).

Name All 50

Can your kids put their brains together and name all 50 states?

Here's a cheat sheet so that you can check off the ones they've gotten and provide some hints for the ones they haven't (like, "There are eight states that begin with the letter *M*.").

Alabama	Hawaii
Alaska	Idaho
Arizona	Illinois
Arkansas	Indiana
California	Iowa
Colorado	Kansas
Connecticut	Kentucky
Delaware	Louisiana
Florida	Maine
Georgia	Maryland

Massachusetts
Michigan
Minnesota
Mississippi
Missouri
Montana
Nebraska
Nevada
New Hampshire
New Jersey
New Mexico
New York
North Carolina
North Dakota
Ohio

Oklahoma
Oregon
Pennsylvania
Rhode Island
South Carolina
South Dakota
Tennessee
Texas
Utah
Vermont
Virginia
Washington
West Virginia
Wisconsin
Wyoming

Two Truths and a Lie

Everyone takes turns making three statements about themselves or their experiences, two that are true and one that is a lie. Because it's likely you know quite a bit about one another, you'll have to say things like, "Yesterday, I saw someone walking down the street dressed like a pirate" or "A skunk was cornered in the school gym today." Try to figure out which of the three statements is a lie!

(Younger children can make just one statement, and the others can guess whether it is the truth or a lie.)

Name That Tune

No game show host required! Just start la-la-la-ing a tune until someone guesses what it is. Start by singing three notes, then four notes, then five, until someone names that tune!

It Was a Dark and Stormy Night . . .

Gather half a dozen or so items, like a penny, a pair of glasses, a lipstick, a stick of gum . . .

Ask the kids to make up a short story incorporating all of the items. They can't leave anything out! They can either take turns building on the same story or tell an entire story one at a time.

I'm Going on a Trip

Here's a fun word game you can play anywhere: "I'm going on a trip. I will bring cheese and tools, but not milk and snacks. Why not?"

Everyone must try to figure out what *cheese* and *tools* have in common that *milk* and *snacks* don't. In this case, the answer is double vowels (*ee* and *oo*).

Another example would be: "I'm going on a trip. I will bring a cat and a rug, but not a puppy or a suitcase." (Answer: You are bringing things with only three letters.)

Clap Trap

Choose a topic: animals, food, clothing. A parent begins listing items, some of which fall under the chosen category and some of which don't. Children have to clap their hands when the item belongs to the category and slap their thighs when it doesn't. You can speed up the game as kids get better at it.

Chief

The more children playing
this game, the more fun it is!
One child closes her eyes
while a parent silently chooses
another child to be the Chief.
Just before the child opens her
eyes, the Chief begins a random
series of movements—clapping,
stamping, twirling, or whatever
your surroundings permit—
and the others immediately
repeat the movements.
The child whose eyes
were closed must
guess who the
Chief is.

TV Titles

One child (or a parent) is designated as the guesser. The others secretly agree on the name of a television show that has as many words in the title as there are players. The guesser asks the first player any random question: "What did you eat for lunch?" or "How was school today?" Within the answer to the question, the player must slip in the first word of the television show. If the show is *Sesame Street*, for example, the player may answer the first sample question with, "Lunch was great, except that I got a sesame seed stuck in between my teeth and I couldn't get it out!"  The next player answers another question with a sentence or two containing the second word in the title. It is the guesser's job to try to figure out which word in each person's answer is part of the television title and eventually to guess the title.

Note: You can also try this with book or movie titles.

The Mirror

Remember the *I Love Lucy* episode in which Lucy pretends to be a mirror reflection and mimics the moves of Harpo Marx? Have two kids face each other and instruct one  to begin moving slowly and the other to try to "mirror" his actions.

Head Massage

Even the squirmiest kid will sit still for a head rub if it's done the right way. Use your spread fingers to gently rub your child's scalp. Run your fingers through her hair and end by running your fingers up the nape of her neck and then massaging upward through her hair until you reach the top of her head. Instant tingles!

Groupies

Can you guess
what kinds of
animals gather
in these various
groups?

- a knot of _____(toads)

- a nursery of _____(raccoons)

- a kit of _____(pigeons)

- a rookery of_____(penguins)

- a company of _____(parrots)

- a parliament of _____(owls)

- a pride of _____ (lions)

- a murder of _____ (crows)

- a smack of _____ (jellyfish)

- a crash of _____ (rhinos)

- a parade of _____ (elephants)

- a peep of _____ (chicks)

- a clutter of _____ (cats)

- a mischief of _____ (rats)

- a gaggle of _____ (geese)

- a shrewdness of _____ (apes)

- a rafter of _____ (turtles)

Drop It and Flip-flop It!

Teach your kids this neat coin trick. Sandwich a nickel between two quarters and hold the coins between your thumb and first finger as shown.

With your other hand 10 inches or so below the coins, let the bottom quarter and the nickel fall while holding onto the top quarter. Amazingly, the two coins will change places as they fall, landing with the nickel under the quarter!

Stick 'Em Up!

Tell your child that something amazing will happen if he stands in a doorway and pushes his hands (hard!) against the sides of the door frame (arms straight, pressing with the backs of his hands) while counting to 45. When he reaches the magic number, have him step forward and pretend that his arms are as light as butterfly wings. He'll be astounded at how his arms seem to float upward as if featherlight!

The Amazing Rubber Pencil

You've probably seen this one before, but it's deceptively tricky to master. Lightly hold a pencil at the eraser end between your thumb and index finger. As you quickly bounce the pencil up and down, it should appear to others as if it is made of rubber. Pass it around to see who can repeat the illusion.

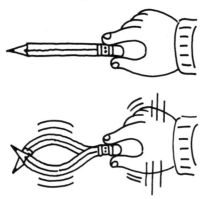

Lousy Luck

Can you guess what the experts say
you should do if:

- a tarantula is clinging to you?
  (Stand up and gently bounce up
  and down until it falls off.)

- a black bear is coming at you?
  (Throw rocks at it and make
  growling noises.)

- a rhino notices you?
  (Stay quiet and still.)

- killer bees are chasing you? (Run!)

- a mountain lion is approaching?
  (Hold your coat open and remain
  still. This will make you look bigger
  and more threatening.)

Penny Catch

See if your child can master the Penny Catch. When she extends her right arm straight out (at shoulder height), place one or more pennies on the inside of her elbow. As she lets her arm drop quickly down to her side, how many pennies can she catch in her right hand?

Penny Puzzler

Make a triangle (like the one shown below) with ten pennies.

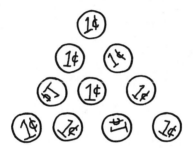

Can the kids move only three pennies and make the triangle point down rather than up?

ANSWER:

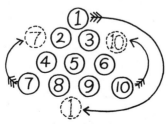

Never Been Played Before

Encourage your kids to invent their own game. Suggest using certain props at hand and ask what kind of game they could create using the assigned props.

School on the Run

Squeeze in a few lessons while you're waiting with your kids. Teach them:

- left from right
- to tie their shoes
- odd numbers and even numbers
- polite phone manners
- how to make change or count money
- to write their names in cursive
- how to braid
- adding and subtracting using items at hand
- how to count to ten in French: *un, deux, trois, quatre, cinq, six, sept, huit, neuf, dix*

True or False?

Tell your kids this tale and then ask them to tell you whether it is true or false—and why:

My friend Mary told me a story recently. She went with her husband, Joe, to the opera.  Joe, who never liked opera, fell asleep right away and started dreaming. He dreamed that he had gone back in time hundreds of years and was condemned to death for a crime he didn't commit. In his dream, his neck was on the block and the guillotine blade had started to fall. Just then the opera reached a dramatic peak, and Mary tapped Joe on the back of the neck to wake him up. Because of the dream he was having, Joe died instantly from a heart attack. Mary feels just terrible about this.

ANSWER: The story is false. Joe died without waking up, so no one could have known what he had been dreaming about!

Chat

Everyone secretly takes on the identity of a famous person. These characters can be sports stars, famous people from history, actors, politicians—anyone who is well known to everyone in the group.

Then the Chat begins, with each person playing the part of the person they've chosen. They ask each other questions, talk about their own achievements, and after an agreed upon length of time try to guess everyone's identity.

Act Out an Adverb

One person covers his ears while the others agree on an adverb they will all act out. As the guesser tries to figure out the adverb, he can request that the players do certain things—eat, sing, walk—to act out the chosen adverb. Try some toughies: hysterically, suspiciously, aggressively . . .

TIP: By the time kids are eight or nine years old, they are often able to keep themselves occupied with a portable CD player or GameBoy. But you may be pleasantly surprised at how quickly they'll jump at the chance to play a family game. And with preteens, it is even more important to connect with them during the little bits of time you have here and there—it may be all you get.

Ripley's Believe It or Not!

Were the following amazing stories of survival reported by *Ripley's Believe It or Not!* . . . or weren't they?

A flight attendant survived after falling 33,000 feet when the plane she was in exploded.

(Yes! It happened in 1972 on a flight over Czechoslovakia.)

When the ship *The Adventurer* sank in Lake Michigan, the only survivor was a man named Samuel Stone, who climbed into a coffin and floated to shore.

(No! It never happened.)

A baby who was kidnapped and kept aboard a yacht floated ashore unharmed after a storm sank the boat and all of the kidnappers drowned.

(Yes! One-and-a-half-year-old Renée Nivernas of France was kidnapped in 1908 and held for ransom. After a storm destroyed the yacht, she floated safely ashore in a cradle made out of packing cases.)

A two-year-old boy from Uganda wandered into the forest near his village and was presumed dead. But he was found years later living in a tree with a family of monkeys.

(Yes! John Ssebunya lived with a family of monkeys until he was found at age six by a villager who noticed him as she was gathering firewood. He was brought to an orphanage, where he learned how to live as a typical little boy, playing soccer and singing in a choir.)

Entries above are from *Ripley's Believe It or Not!* Special Edition, by Mary Packard and the editors of Ripley Entertainment (Scholastic, 2001).

The Quaker Meeting

One child announces to the others: "The Quaker meeting is about to begin. There will be absolutely no noise, *especially* laughter." Then she proceeds to do everything she can—make funny faces or funny sounds, tell jokes—to make someone laugh. If she is able to elicit a giggle within one minute, she can dole out a punishment to the giggler (a punishment might be taking up the garbage if you are at a fast-food restaurant, for instance, or doing ten jumping jacks). If she is not able to make anyone laugh, the others decide what *her* punishment will be!

The Riddler

Tell your older kids these tales and see if they can figure out what happened. They are allowed to ask you questions, but only those that can be answered with a yes or a no.

1. Four men are found dead in a cabin in the woods. What happened?

2. Two children stand looking up at a ball in a tree, but they make no attempt to get it down. Why not?

3. A man leaves home, takes a left, a left, and another left, and is confronted by a masked man. What happened?

ANSWERS: 1. A plane crashed in the woods, killing the men on board, whose bodies are still in the plane's cabin. 2. It is a decoration on a Christmas tree. 3. He is a baseball player who just hit a home run.

Guess the Category

Think of a category (or use one from the list below) and begin naming things that would fall within that category. For instance, you might start by saying, "Pants . . . shirts . . . shoes . . . belts . . . a birthday present you don't want anyone to see . . . a laundry basket." See how quickly the others can guess, "Things people keep in their closets."

A few other category ideas:

- things that break if you drop them

- things Mom (or Dad or Baby) refuses to eat

- things that are hard

- things that might be in the trunk of a car

- things that are squishy

- things people throw in the trash

- things people often lose

- things people might find under the sofa cushions

- things people are likely to borrow from one another

- things that make people laugh

- things people tell the doctor

Country Classics

Are these actual titles of country songs . . . or not? Your older kids will have fun trying to guess.

"How Come Your Dog Don't Bite Nobody but Me?" *(Yes!)*

"If Today Was a Fish, I'd Throw It Back." *(Yes!)*

"My Horse Loves You So I Guess I Will Too." *(No)*

"I Like Bananas Because They Have No Bones." *(Yes!)*

"Martians Stole My Favorite Cow." *(No)*

"If the Phone Doesn't Ring, It's Me." *(Yes!)*

"How Can I Miss You if You Won't Go Away?" *(Yes!)*

"How Can You Forget What I Never Even Said?" *(No)*

"Walk Out Backwards Slowly So I'll Think You're Walking In." *(Yes!)*

World Records

Can your kids fill
in the blanks of
these feats listed

recently on the *Guinness Book of World Records* Web site?

France's Michael Lotito has been eating 2 pounds of _____ every day since 1959.   (ANSWER: metal)

Californian Gary Hardwick set a speed record in 1998 by going 62.5 miles per hour on a _____.
(ANSWER: skateboard, in a standing position)

At 15 inches across, this _____ found in Montana in 1887 was the largest ever measured.   (ANSWER: snowflake)

In 1965, baseball player "Satchel" Paige pitched for the Kansas City A's when he was _____ years old.

(ANSWER: 59)

The windiest place in the world, with a 231-mile-per-hour wind recorded in April 1934, is _____.

(ANSWER: Mount Washington in New Hampshire)

Vivian Wheeler of Illinois holds the record for the longest _____, at 11 feet (as of 2000).

(ANSWER: female beard)

What body part of Shridhar Chillal has a combined length of 20 feet, 2 inches?

(ANSWER: five fingernails on his left hand)

When he was ten years old, Michael Kearney became the youngest person to _____.

(ANSWER: graduate from college—the University of Southern Alabama with a B.A. in anthropology)

3 Ways to Play with a Dollar Bill

Kids love to play with money. Here are three fun things to do with a dollar bill:

1. Turn It Upside Down

Hold a dollar bill so that the president's face is looking at you. Fold the top half of the dollar bill down, then fold the left half of the bill away from you, toward the right. Unfold the half

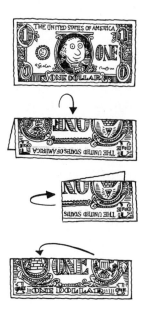

of the bill facing you toward the
left. Unfold the bill so that the
president's face is looking at you
upside down!

2. Pick It Up and It's Yours!

Tell your child that if he can pick
up a dollar bill, it's his! He must
stand with his back and heels
against a wall. If he can pick up
a dollar bill placed a foot or so in
front of him without moving his
heels or bending his knees, it's his!

3. Paper Clip Connection

Beg two paper clips from a nearby receptionist or hostess. Slip the paper clips onto the dollar bill as shown. When you grab the ends of the bill and yank it taut, the paper clips will link together!

Penny Picker

Challenge each of your kids in turn to this seemingly simple game—and tell them you guarantee you'll always win. Then show them how it's done!

Lay out 20 pennies on a flat surface. Tell the kids that the object of the game is to take turns picking up pennies (either one, two, or three at a time) until someone picks up the last penny—that person is the winner!

Here's how to win every time: Have the other player go first. Then see that for each turn the combined number of pennies picked up is four. In other words, if he picks up three, you pick up one. If he picks up two, *you* pick up two. When round five comes, there will be four pennies left. No matter how many the other player takes—one, two, or three—you will be left with the last penny!

Number Magic

Tell your kids that they had better be careful: You can read minds! Here's what you say: "Think of a secret number, but don't make it too big because you'll have to do some adding, dividing, and subtracting. First, add to your number the next highest number (if your number is 10, add 11). Now add 9. Divide this number by 2. Now subtract your original number. The answer you will get is . . . 5!"

You will always be right because the answer will always be 5!

Staring Contests

Especially good if you want your kids to sit still for an extended period of time, staring contests have the simplest of rules: Don't blink and don't look away. Whoever outlasts the other wins!

What Is It?

Take turns passing something
around the group—a book, a
mitten, a shoe. Every time the
item changes hands, the person
who receives it decides what it
is. Without speaking, he reacts
to the item in such a way that
the others can guess its identity.
Maybe he rocks it in his arms
because it's a baby, or tosses
it quickly from hand to hand
because it's a hot potato, or has
trouble holding it because it's a
very heavy rock. When someone
guesses correctly, the item is
passed along.

Finger Power

Let your kids in on a little secret: You have a special power that allows you to mentally force people's fingers to move! Have one of your children clasp her hands tightly together (with interwoven fingers) and then lift her index fingers straight up and as far apart as she can.

Now wave your hands over hers and command her index fingers to come together. They will—but not because of you; they just aren't able to stay in the other position very long!

The Talking Stick

Find something resembling a stick (anything from a pencil to a paper towel tube will do). Someone in the group holds the stick and begins to tell a story. After a sentence or two, he passes the stick to the person of his choosing, who continues the story until she passes the stick to someone else. No one can refuse to take the stick!

Tic-Tac-Toe with a Twist

Make a traditional tic-tac-toe grid, but then play it backwards: Any player with three-in-a-row *Os* or *Xs* *loses* rather than wins! (If you are in a restaurant, you can make the grid with coffee stirrers and use sugar and sugar substitute packets as your *Xs* and *Os*!)

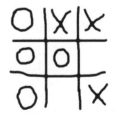

Amazing Animals

Can your kids complete these amazing animal facts?

_____ have killed more people than any other wild animal.

ANSWER: Hippos

Birds do not _____ in their nests.

ANSWER: sleep

The platypus is the only mammal that is _____.

ANSWER: poisonous

Instead of barking when it gets excited, a dog called the basenji usually _____.

ANSWER: yodels

Ship captains used to keep _____ on board because they believed that if the boat sank, these smart animals would swim toward the nearest shore.

ANSWER: pigs

_____ can carry ten times their body weight.

ANSWER: Ants

The most poisonous _____ is the size of a golf ball and can kill a human being in minutes.

ANSWER: octopus

The largest _____ is as big as a baby deer.

ANSWER: frog

Who Wants to Be a Millionaire?

If your child answers these questions correctly, she may be ready for prime time! (The answer is the choice in italics.)

The _____ is the world's most popular fruit.

a. apple   **b.** *tomato*
c. banana   **d.** orange

A fresh egg will _____, but a stale one won't.

a. break easily
b. roll in a straight line
c. *sink in water*
d. have a speckled shell

Over 5 billion _____ are made for kids every year.

a. *crayons* **b.** yo-yos

c. pop-up books **d.** baseball trading cards

Eighty percent of Americans have _____ in their cupboards.

a. spaghetti sauce

b. chicken noodle soup

c. *oatmeal*

d. honey

One in every ten people in the world lives on _____.

a. *an island*

b. Main Street

c. top of an ancient burial site

d. a farm

_____ was invented 48 years after canned foods were introduced.

a. The label **b.** *The can opener*

c. Frozen food **d.** Spam

Clapping and Rhyming Games

Here's a set of games that may remind you of your childhood. Girls especially like to singsong these rhymes to a repeated pattern of clapping, finger snapping, knee slapping (in a sequence of their choosing). Here are some favorites:

A sailor went to sea, sea, sea,
To see what he could see, see, see.
But all that he could see, see, see,
Was the bottom of the deep blue sea,
     sea, sea.

★ ★ ★ ★ ★ ★ ★ ★ ★ ★ ★

Coca-Cola went to town;
Pepsi-Cola shot him down.
Dr. Pepper fixed him up and
Changed him into Bubble Up.

A horse, a flea, and three blind mice
Sat on a curbstone shooting dice.
The horse, he slipped and fell on the flea.
The flea said, "Whoops! There's a horse
    on me!"

★ ★ ★ ★ ★ ★ ★ ★ ★ ★ ★

Miss Mary Mack, Mack, Mack,
All dressed in black, black, black,
With silver buttons, buttons, buttons,
All down her back, back, back.
She asked her mother, mother, mother,
For fifty cents, cents, cents,
To see the elephants, elephants,
    elephants,
Jump over the fence, fence, fence.
They jumped so high, high, high,
They touched the sky, sky, sky,
And didn't come back, back, back,
Till the fourth of July, July, July.

I Spy

The Old Faithful of waiting games, I Spy still appeals to kids, especially younger ones. Someone spots an item of interest and begins the game by saying, "I spy with my little eye something . . . blue!" Each person takes one guess and then she offers another clue, such as, "I spy with my little eye something blue and fuzzy!" Whoever guesses correctly is the next one to spy.

What If . . .

Kids love to ponder issues like these: What if a genie appeared and offered you three wishes?

What if you won 10 million dollars?

What if you could choose any animal from the zoo to be your pet?

What if you could visit any place in the universe?

What if you could be someone else for a day (but you didn't get to choose whom)?

What if you could choose any special power to have?

What if you had to choose to be either gigantic or tiny for one day?

Clap, Clap, Snap, Snap

Players begin by sitting down and establishing this pattern: clapping both hands on the thighs twice, clapping hands together twice, snapping fingers on the left hand once, then snapping fingers on the right hand once. After they've practiced that sequence a few times, someone names a category (on the snap, snap) like states or baseball teams or television shows. Each player, in turn, names something that fits the category on the double snap part of the sequence. If someone can't name anything, repeats a previous answer, or names something that doesn't fit, he's out.

20-Second Challenge

If your watch has a second hand, offer to count how many times in a 20-second period your child can:

- snap his fingers

- cluck his tongue

- flare his nostrils

- wink

- hop on one foot

- do jumping jacks

- _____ (your choice)

If Winks Could Kill

This is an especially good game to play when you need to keep a group of kids sitting quietly. All of the children close their eyes while an adult secretly taps one of them on the head. This child becomes the Winker. He kills off the players one at a time by winking at them, though he must do it without the others seeing him. As soon as someone is winked at, she slumps over and plays dead. If anyone witnesses him winking and says, "He's the Winker!" the jig is up! (But anyone who guesses wrong is out!)

Family-arity

How well do you know the people in your family? Can you name everyone's:

- best friend

- favorite song

- favorite movie

- happiest moment

- favorite place for a vacation

- most embarrassing moment

- favorite time of the year

- ideal pet

- least favorite food

- favorite spot in the house

Word Association

Just like patients in a sitcom psychiatrist's office, players are required to quickly call out the first thing that comes into their minds when the leader says a word. After everyone has made an association, the person to the leader's right has to repeat everyone's answers. If she does so correctly, she becomes the new leader.

A variation: The second player responds to the word of the first player, then the third player responds to the word of the second player, and so on. A player who hesitates is out. The last player left wins!

A second variation: Someone calls out a number ("Three!"), and the first person to make an association ("Three French hens!") becomes the next one to call out a number!

Sing Along

Take turns singing
the first line of a
popular song, then
pointing to another
person who must sing
the second line. Anyone who is
stumped is out.

Note: Don't try this with teenagers.
A popular song to you would not
be popular with them!

restaurant games

Every seasoned parent has
lived through a restaurant
nightmare with the kids
squirming and whining (or worse) as
childless people at nearby tables
grumble and stare.

Restaurants offer myriad game
options, from quiet to more
boisterous,
cerebral to just
plain goofy. The
fact that
everyone is
seated together
at a table facing
one another

makes it easy to engage the whole group. Following are the games that parents say work best. (These ideas don't require any further props than are found in most casual restaurants [straws, salt shakers, place mats], but if you're inclined to make a restaurant Bag of Tricks, see page 318 for ideas.)

Pass!

Everyone at the table turns over a paper place mat and begins to draw. When Mom or Dad says, "Pass to the right!" everyone does just that. Kids continue the drawing that has been passed to them until the next "Pass to the right!" command. After the drawings have made the rounds a couple of times, hold each one up for all to see!

Pass Blindly!

This is similar to the game of Pass!
but in this version you will all
agree ahead of time what animal
or person to draw. The first person
will draw the body, the second
the head, the third the arms and
legs . . .

The catch: You keep your eyes
closed until your part of the
drawing is complete—
only then can you
examine your
collective (and
undoubtedly
odd) creature.

Pass Folded!

Fold a piece of paper into thirds. The first person will draw a head on the top third of the paper with the bottom lines just crossing the crease. He will fold his drawing back so that the next player can't see it as he adds a body. The third person will add legs and feet without knowing what the others have drawn. When she is done, the paper is unfolded and the masterpiece is revealed!

Read My Mind

This game is terrific for a lively and creative group. Start everyone off with five sugar packets. One person thinks of a noun—any noun. Everyone else makes a random guess as to what the noun may be. When all have guessed, the first player announces her word, and the others must all explain how the words they guessed relate to the secret word. For instance, if the secret noun was *chair* and the guess was *horse,* the guesser could say that both have four legs and a person sitting on them. Each explanation is given a thumbs-up or thumbs-down by the other players. A majority of thumbs-downs means the guesser loses one sugar packet. If everyone gets a thumbs-down on a given round, the player who thought of the secret word forfeits a sugar packet. The person with the most sugar packets left wins.

Restaurant Rubbings

With the crayons often supplied by forward-thinking restaurants, make rubbings with whatever you have at hand: coins, credit cards, keys . . . All you need to do is place your place mat or a piece of paper over the item and rub the crayon across it.

Lip Reading

If those orders of chicken fingers
are taking longer than everyone
anticipated, see if there are any
talented lip readers in your group.
Take turns mouthing a sentence
to those sitting across the table.
Can anyone figure out what you
are saying?

Doodles

Ahhh! Here's a little game that will take you back to your childhood: Take turns drawing simple doodles on each other's paper place mats or napkins. Now turn the doodles into something (or someone) recognizable!

A variation: Rather than making a squiggly doodle for someone to turn into a picture, make a series of dots that another person must connect and turn into a person or object.

Folding Challenge

Can you fold your paper place mat in half? How about in half again? Easy, right? Challenge your kids to try folding their place mats in half more than eight times. It can't be done, but this challenge will use up some critical waiting time!

Fast-Food Magic Trick

You can play this game at restaurants that have stacks of small paper cups for condiments or water. Wad up a straw's paper wrapper and stick it under an upside-down cup. Add two or three other upside-down cups (more if your kids are older to make the game harder), and then slide the cups around the table quickly so that everyone watching loses sight of which cup is hiding the straw paper. If someone guesses correctly after a minute or two of cup shuffling, it's his or her turn next!

Order Up!

You don't need to wait
for the server to begin
ordering your food! Start
with someone at your table
ordering one item. The
person to her right repeats
her order, then adds an item.
The third person repeats
the orders of the first two,
then adds his own item.
It may seem easy at first,
but wait until you've gone
around the table a few times!

Fun with Water Glasses

When your food is still MIA and the kids have lost interest in the more cerebral restaurant games, you may need to resort to activities such as these:

1. Ask everyone to drink their water down to a different level. With your utensils, tap water glasses to create a symphony.

2. Fill a water glass to the top, then continue adding spoonfuls carefully, watching as the water rises above the side of the glass.

3. Using only two straws (like chopsticks), try to fish an ice cube out of your water glass. The one who manages to pull out the biggest ice cube is the winner!

4. Drop a dime into a water glass. Now try to drop a penny into the glass so that it will completely cover up the dime.

5. Make faces at each other through your water glasses.

6. Choose a few items on the table (straw wrapper, sugar packet, scrap of place mat), and guess whether or not they will float. Drop each one into a glass of water to see if you were right.

Quick Draw

With the crayons often provided at family restaurants, you can fool the kids into thinking you have eyes in the back of your head.

Spread the crayons on the table and turn your back. Tell the kids to select one crayon and hide the others. Cup your hands behind your back to receive the chosen crayon. As you turn back toward the table, secretly scribble on your thumbnail with the crayon. Bring the marked hand casually onto the table, continuing to hold the crayon behind your back with the other hand. Glance down at the color on your thumbnail and "guess" the color of the crayon!

Knot Likely

Lay someone's shoelace on the table. Challenge one of the kids to tightly grab hold of each end and tie a knot in it—without loosening either of his fists. Just before utter frustration sets in,  show him how to do it: Cross your arms in front of you and grab an end with each hand. Without letting go, uncross your arms and the shoelace will have a knot in it!

Blow It Up!

Have the kids open up their napkins and tear out the shape of something that flies— a butterfly, a bird, a plane . . . Now tell them to toss their napkin shapes into the air and

TIP: Order your child's meal as soon as you are seated and ask that it be brought out as soon as it is ready. She'll be much easier to entertain if she's not hungry and cranky.

blow through their straws to see if they can keep them up!

Pass Me a Menu

Reach under the table and put a menu between your feet. Without looking, pass it from one person's feet to another's until someone drops it. He's out, and the game continues until you have a winner.

Backward R-E-L-L-E-P-S

Begin spelling an item from the menu backwards. Who will be the first one to guess what it is?

6 Ways to Have Messy Fun in a Restaurant

Watch how fast the food will be delivered to your table when the server catches a glimpse of your family engaged in one of these waiting games:

1. Shine up your tarnished pennies with ketchup.

2. Balance a salt shaker on some grains of salt: Dump a little salt on the table. Balance the salt shaker at an angle on one

of its flat edges in the pile. When it balances without being held, gently blow away the extra salt and—why, it's magic!

3. Dump a little sugar and salt onto a dish or your place mat. Wet a tine of your fork (or a coffee stirrer) and dip it in the sugar, then touch different parts of your tongue (afterward, do the same with salt). Which parts of your tongue can taste sweet and which parts can taste salty?

4. Dribble water on your paper place mat and blow on it through your straw to create a masterpiece.

5. Dump a little salt and pepper on a dish or a place mat and mix it up. Now rub a straw back and forth on your sweater. Have the kids guess what will happen when you hold the straw above the salt and pepper. (The pepper attaches to the straw before the salt does because it is lighter.)

6. Make an ice cube tower using salt to help the ice cubes stick together.

Spelling Bee

Using the menu as a source for spelling words, take turns giving each other words, with points accruing for each correct spelling: Five points gets an extra special drink (a Shirley Temple or an Oreo shake); ten points equals any dessert on the menu!

(As an added challenge, have the person sitting across from the speller guess "Right!" or "Wrong!" after the spelling attempt. He can win an extra point if he's correct!)

Create-a-Crossword

On the back of the place mats, draw crossword puzzle grids that are five squares by five squares. Then go around the table and take turns calling out letters. Everyone must write every letter somewhere, the object being to make as many five-letter words as possible.

Before the Leftovers . . .

As you are being seated, ask the host or hostess to bring you a Styrofoam container used for packing leftovers.

Take turns secretly putting something inside the container. The others must guess what's inside based on holding or shaking the container. They are not permitted to ask questions and are allowed just one guess each. As a variation, you can try to guess how many of something are inside.

TIP: If you are on vacation, use the waiting time in a restaurant to write out postcards to friends and family. Some kids like to write postcards to themselves to remind them of the things they saw or did. Once home, they punch a hole in the corner of each postcard and join them all with a metal ring.

6 Great Games with Sugar Packets

1. Assign the differently colored sugar and sugar substitute packets various monetary values. Close your eyes and divvy them up among the kids, then let them add up the total to see who is the richest!

2. Make a tower of sugar packets, taking turns adding them one at a time. Whoever is responsible for the tower's downfall (usually more of a downslide) loses!

3. Give everyone five sugar packets. At "Go!" everyone begins handing out packets to the others— as many or as few as they would like. (No one can refuse to accept a sugar packet.) After a few minutes of trading, say "Stop!" and then call out a number (from one up to the number of packets in play). Everyone counts how many packets he has in hand, and whoever is closest wins.

4. Empty a sugar packet and pass it around the table using only your straws: Put the packet at the end of your straw and suck in to keep it in place, then transfer it to the next person's straw without dropping it!

5. Hold up your hand, palm down, and see how many sugar packets you can stack on it.

6. Lay several sugar packets on the table and take turns flipping pennies off your thumb from the table's edge, trying to make them land on a packet.

Presto-Chango!

Each person at the table writes
down two three-letter words on
the paper place mat of the person
to the right. Now everyone must
turn the first word into the second
word by changing one letter at a
time, creating a new word each
time.

As an example: COT NAP would
become cot . . . cat . . . cap . . . nap.
The winner is the one who changes
the first word into the second in
the least number of steps.

Pass the Penny

One child is the guesser while the others are the passers. Underneath the table, they pass a penny from person to person. After a predetermined amount of time— perhaps 30 seconds or until the server brings the drinks—the guesser says "Stop!" and everyone puts clenched fists on top of the table. The guesser points to the person she thinks is holding the penny (to make it tougher, require the person to choose the correct hand). If she's right, she becomes one of the passers, and the person she fingered guesses.

Straw Ball

Take the paper wrapper off a straw and ball it up. Take turns blowing through your straw at the paper ball so that it shoots across the table but stops before falling off the edge. The kid who gets closest to the edge without going over wins!

A variation: With everyone at the table equipped with a straw, teams on each side try to blow the straw-paper ball through salt-and-pepper-shaker goalposts on the other side of the table. Whoever scores five goals first wins!

Spoon Fun

1. Hang a spoon on the end of your nose.

2. Make faces at your reflection in a spoon. (Does it look different when you turn the spoon over?)

3. Pass a packet of sugar from one person's spoon to another's without dropping it. The hitch: Hold the spoon handles in your mouths!

4. Play the spoons: Put two spoons back-to-back and tuck them on either side of your middle finger. Then strum the spoons with the other hand and hit them against your knee.

5. Play Musical Spoons: Place one fewer spoons than players in the middle of the table. One person closes her eyes and starts humming or whistling. The minute she stops, everyone grabs for a spoon. The one without a spoon is out, and one more spoon is removed from the table. Play on until you have a winner!

6. Guess what the spoon is tapping: While everyone else at the table closes their eyes, one person taps her spoon on something nearby. The others have to guess what it is.

Silly Sentences

A parent calls out four random letters. The children have a minute or two to write a sentence on the back of their place mats in which the words begin with the letters in the order given. So the letters *T-B-A-R* could be "The bunny ate radishes" or "Two beasts are roaming." After the kids have read their sentences aloud, they are ready for another series of letters.

Pick-Up Sticks

Here's an impromptu restaurant version of an old favorite: Grab a handful of coffee stirrers and hold them 8 to 10 inches above the table. Drop them in a pile and then take turns trying to remove one without moving any of the others. If you are successful, you can keep the stick and continue your turn. If not, the next person takes a turn. Whoever ends up with the most sticks at game's end wins!

After-Dinner Activities

If you ordered your
kids' meals first,
chances are
you're still eating
long after they're done.
To keep younger kids busy, have
them turn the leftovers on their
plates into a face. Older kids can
guess the final bill by adding up
the items ordered from the menu.
Then they can figure out what the
tip should be.

Boxes

In this familiar game, someone turns over her paper place mat and draws ten rows of ten dots that line up vertically and horizontally. Two players take turns connecting any two dots that are next to each other (no diagonal lines can be drawn). The goal is to be the one who connects the final two dots to complete a box. That person puts her initial in the box. Each time she completes a box, she can take an extra turn. The person who has completed the most boxes when every line has been drawn is the winner.

Napkin Puzzler

Assuming you can get more napkins, have all the kids rip their folded napkins into a few pieces. Now ask them to open up the pieces, save one, and mix the others up in the middle of the table. Can everyone put their puzzle napkins together?

Toothpick Puzzler

Using toothpicks (or coffee stirrers), create a grid like the one shown here:

Now try to solve the following puzzles:

Can you move only three toothpicks and turn the four separate areas into three of equal size (using all of the toothpicks)?

Can you turn the grid into two squares by taking away just two toothpicks?

ANSWERS:

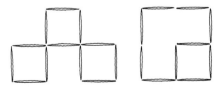

Place Mat Projects

When the cerebral games have lost their appeal, you can resort to turning the place mats (or pieces of them) into toys.

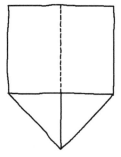

Make a paper airplane:

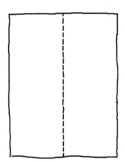

1. Fold along centerline and reopen.

2. Fold bottom corners as shown.

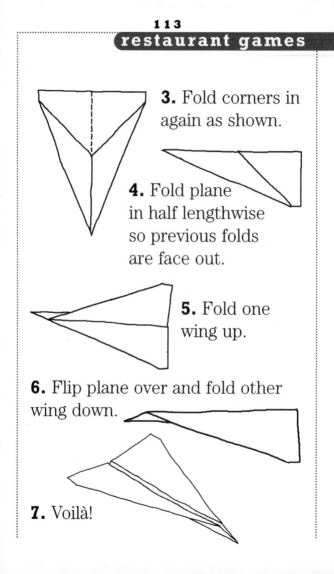

3. Fold corners in again as shown.

4. Fold plane in half lengthwise so previous folds are face out.

5. Fold one wing up.

6. Flip plane over and fold other wing down.

7. Voilà!

restaurant games

Make a twirly:

1. Fold and tear a strip of your place mat about an inch wide and 10 to 12 inches long. About an inch from each end, tear halfway through the strip.

2. Slip one end into the other as shown.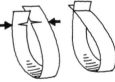

3. Hold the twirly above your head, release it, and watch it spin to the ground.

Make a paper popper:

1. Fold and tear your place mat to make a square of about 6 inches: Fold in half along a diagonal and reopen.

2. Fold the square in half along the other diagonal and reopen.

3. Fold in half along the center as shown.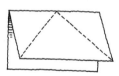

4. Fold opposite sides inwards as shown.

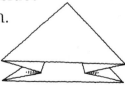

5. Hold popper between your thumb and middle finger, with your index finger tucked in the fold as shown. Snap your arm downward to make a pop!

Change'll Do You Good

Put some coins into a paper
cup. Put your hand over
the top and shake the cup.
If someone can guess
the exact amount
of change, she
can have the
money! Change
the amount
of money
and play
again!

Restaurant Tricks

Teach your kids these tricks that will amaze and amuse their friends!

The Invisible Penny Trick

Fill a water glass to the brim and cover the top with a saucer. Now carefully lift and place the glass on top of a penny. Hey! No more penny! (This works best if the base of the glass isn't too thick.)

A Straw Deal

Put two drinking straws in your mouth. Then put the end of one in a glass of water or soda, keeping the end of the other outside the glass. Bet you can't sip anything through the straw! (And no fair covering the end of the straw that's not in the drink!)

Triple Rip

Fold a paper place mat into thirds and open it up again. Tear along each fold until you are an inch or so from the top of the placemat. Holding along the top corners of the place mat, try to pull the paper evenly so that both of the tears go completely through the paper simultaneously, leaving the middle piece to drop out. Guess what? It can't be done! One side will tear completely!

Telephone with a Twist

You can play Telephone the way you did as a kid—whispering a complicated phrase from one kid to another until the final player announces the (much-altered) phrase—or you can play the updated version.

Instead of sending a phrase through the group, send an image. Secretly draw a simple sketch on a piece of paper (like the back of a restaurant place mat). The next child has a few seconds to look at the drawing, then draws her version and shows it to the third person. When everyone has had a turn, compare the last drawing with the original one for a good chuckle!

Telephone with a Double Twist

Play traditional Telephone, but send two different messages— one in each direction around the circle. The messages will cross somewhere in the circle and, once each has been heard and repeated by every child, will be voiced out loud in an undoubtedly mangled form.

. . . And a Triple Twist

Make a face at the person next to you, who repeats the face to the person next to her, and so on. Don't forget to compare the first and last faces!

Eavesdrop

There's no better way to get your kids to be absolutely quiet than to tell them to listen to what is being said at nearby tables; then they can try to guess what is going on based on the snippets of conversation. Guide your kids in outrageous directions to make it interesting: Did the man who asked his wife if she had the money just rob a bank? Did the teenager who was talking to his friend about a movie have a starring role? Is he a celebrity?

Snake

Begin by drawing the same pattern of dots as for the game Boxes (page 109). The first player draws a line (horizontal or vertical, not diagonal) to connect two dots. The second player draws a line that connects either end of the first player's line to an adjacent dot. The two players take turns drawing a line from either end of the "snake" to a dot. The object is to continue extending the snake's length while trying to force the other player to draw a line that will *join* to part of the snake.

TIP: At casual, order-at-the-counter-then-sit-down-style restaurants, call ahead and place an order to go, even if you plan on eating at the restaurant. You'll do your waiting at home, then arrive in time to pick up the food and take it to a table to eat.

Hangman

Though the concept may seem a bit morbid by today's standards, Hangman remains a popular game for kids to play. One person thinks of a word and draws one blank for each letter in the word. The other player begins guessing the letters he thinks may be in the secret word. If he guesses correctly, the letter is

TIP: If you have trouble keeping your kids happily corralled while you wait in line to order at a fast-food restaurant, head for the drive-thru. Once you've gotten your food, park, and then take the gang inside to eat.

written in the appropriate blank. If the guess is wrong, the first player begins to draw a hanged man, each part of the drawing representing one incorrect guess. (The incorrect letters are written down also, to avoid repeats.) If the hangman is completed before the second player guesses the word, the first player gets to go again.

_ _ S _

KTPAL

Penny Pushers

Using a quarter as a
target, slide pennies
across the table, trying
to get as close to the
quarter as possible
without actually touching
it. (You can knock your
opponents' pennies out of
the way!) The winner is
the one whose penny
lands closest to the
quarter.

In Disguise

While everyone's eyes are closed, hide something under your napkin (on top of the table). See who can guess what it is.

Coin Roll

Stand two menus up on the table (close to one another) and try to roll pennies between them. An easy game to describe, but not as easy to do!

7 Crazy Ways to Draw

Give each child a pen or pencil from your bag. On the back of a paper place mat they can try drawing pictures or writing words in some nontraditional ways:

1. with the wrong hand

2. with eyes closed

3. looking at the object being drawn, but not at the paper

4. backwards, using a hand mirror from your purse

5. with the pencil between their teeth

6. with the pen attached to another object (perhaps a straw or a spoon), using a hair elastic or a rubber band

7. while they trace a circle on the floor with one foot

car games

I n many cases, you are able to anticipate a potentially tedious drive with your children and plan accordingly. You can pack a bag of toys (see Bag of Tricks, page 310) and plan stops to stretch, use the restroom, and load up on snacks. You can even rent a portable VCR for the drive.

If you have a long drive ahead of you, for instance, you may consider leaving very early in the morning, even before it's light. You can load the car the night before, carry kids from their beds to the car when you're ready to go, and enjoy a few

hours of quiet driving as they sleep.
When they are finally ready for
breakfast, you've already made a
dent in your trip. Some parents
prefer driving through the night while
the kids sleep.

Nonetheless, sometimes your time
in the car is longer than planned or
you overestimated how long the kids
would be entertained by the toys
and snacks you provided. The games
that follow are intended to keep little
passengers happy and busy, while
not distracting the driver too much.
Some work well when the car is
moving; others are better suited to
traffic jams or slow-moving traffic.
(For a few more ideas for car trips,
see page 321.) Have a safe trip!

I Heard It!

Keep kids listening quietly to the radio when you're stuck in traffic by playing I Heard It! Take turns picking a common word you might hear a radio announcer say or a word you might hear in a song (*weather, traffic, song, love* . . .) and award a small prize to the first child who hears it. You can play a variation of this game in which every child chooses a different word (a noun), and the one who hears her word on the radio first wins!

Red Car, Blue Car, Old Car, New Car

Pick two colors from this list: red, blue, silver, black, white, tan, green. The first color you picked is your One-Point Color—every car of that color that passes you or that you pass earns you one point toward your ten-point goal.

Here's the hitch: Your second color is your Cancel Color. If a car that is your Cancel Color passes you or is passed by you before you have amassed ten points, your points are canceled and you have to start all over again!

Rolling Categories

Think of a secret category
(billboards, pickup trucks, cars
with something on the roof . . .)
and count out loud every time
you see something from the car
window that fits into your category.

Everyone else
tries to guess
your secret
category.
The correct
guesser goes
next!

Fast Friends

Award your kids points for getting someone in another vehicle to respond to the following actions:

1. waving a hand

2. waving a foot

3. making a silly face

4. pumping an arm as a sign for a trucker to blow his horn

5. saluting

6. smiling

7. _____ (Add your own action here!)

Author! Author!

Take turns making up stories about the people in the cars that you pass. Who are they? Where are they going? Why are they going there? Who doesn't want to go, and why? What have they brought with them? What will they find when they arrive at their destination?

TIP: To make it less likely that you and your kids will get stuck in a traffic jam, log on to the national traffic information page, fhwa.dot.gov/trafficinfo (a Web site run by the Federal Highway Administration). Click on your state for information about road construction or traffic delays so you can plan accordingly.

My New Car

Take turns picking a number between 5 and 25. Begin counting the cars that pass in the other direction. When you reach the number you chose, that is your new (okay, *pretend* new) car! Who got the nifty sports car and who got the old clunker?

TIP: You can encourage participation in car games by offering coveted prizes, such as the winner gets to:

- choose the radio station
- use the pillow or blanket
- decide whether the windows stay up or down
- determine when to pull over and take a break
- choose the fast-food restaurant
- decide whether or not people in the car can sing with the radio

How Far, How Fast?

Let your kids take turns guessing how long it takes for your car to go one mile. Set the trip meter and say "Start!" Then choose one child to tell you when she thinks a mile has gone by. After she's guessed, tell her what the actual mileage is; then give someone else a turn. You'll be surprised at how quickly they improve at this game! Now have the kids guess how fast the car is going— with their eyes closed! Is anybody close?

License Plate Lottery

On slips of paper, write down a seven-digit number for each child (or let them do this themselves). These are their lottery tickets. The first child to find every number on his ticket by looking at the license plates of cars on the road wins the lottery!

TIP: Give each child 20 nickels (or a handful of change) at the beginning of your trip. Every time a child whines or creates a fuss, take away a nickel (or two or three, depending on the extent of the fuss). When you reach your destination, the kids can keep the nickels they have left.

Familiar Turf

If you are
traveling along
a familiar route,
kids can take
turns closing their eyes and
answering questions from each
other: Do you think we passed
the purple house yet? What
road do you think we're on?
Did we go over the river yet?

Name That Tune: No Singing Required!

To keep older kids engaged, scan the stations on your car radio, pausing briefly on every music station. Can your kids name the song and the artist with only a five-second listen?

TIP: To keep kids from getting cranky, make frequent UNrest stops. Every two hours or so, take a break for a 20-minute romp. Look for community playgrounds or athletic fields, fast-food restaurant playgrounds, or even an emtpy parking lot. Refer to Outside Games (page 227) for ideas for activities. When they get back in the car, have them switch seats just to add a little variety.

Raindrop Race

A rainy car ride means just one
thing to the kids: Raindrop Races!
Each child spots a raindrop that
has landed near the top of his car
window. At "Go!" the children
watch their raindrops as they
make their way down the windows.
(If a chosen raindrop combines
with another along its way, it still
counts.) The owner of the raindrop
that reaches the bottom of the
window first wins!

Car Bingo

Rather than using bingo cards, just play a verbal round or two. Who will be the first one to spot:

• a bike rack with a bike on it

• a school decal in a car window

• their initials on a license plate

• graffiti

• a motorcycle

• a car with a bumper sticker

• a car broken down by the side of the road

• a car with a dog in it

• a car with something on top

- something dangling off a rearview mirror

- a car with at least three kids in it

- a driver wearing a hat

- someone asleep in a car

- a car in which everyone is wearing glasses

TIP:
Sometimes a fussy young child can be calmed just by changing something simple: Try moving him elsewhere in the car, adding or removing clothes, taking off his shoes, turning the radio on or off.

Face-Off

As you prepare to pass the car in front of you, describe what you think the driver will look like based on the kind of car he's driving. You'll be surprised how accurate your description will be based solely on the make, model, and year of the vehicle! (Someone who is not playing can award points between one and ten based on how close the guess is.)

waiting room games

Kids may be hanging in a waiting room for a dental checkup or for your ob-gyn appointment, but most likely they are waiting for a visit with the pediatrician.

To keep waiting to a minimum, pediatricians suggest you schedule Well Child appointments for first thing in the morning or for right after lunch. You're much more likely to be ushered in close to your appointment time.

In addition, call the office before leaving home to find out if the doctor is running late. Ask to speak to the nurse (rather than the receptionist), because she has a better idea of how things are progressing.

Although most waiting rooms have toys for kids to play with, many parents worry about germs. The following games are germfree options for fun as well as distraction from the anxiety that often accompanies a visit to the doctor.

Sucker!

Many waiting areas have bowls or baskets of hard candy, presumably to distract you from the long wait. Stage a suck-off: Give each older child a hard candy and see who can make it last the longest. The only rule? It has to stay in the child's mouth! (They can monitor their progress by looking in a mirror or by describing each other's candy size.) Want to make this game extra hard? Before you start, have the kids put their socks on their hands and then try to unwrap the candy!

Kick a Nickel

Can your child kick a nickel across the waiting room and back? Place one on the floor and challenge her!

Paper Trail

One child stands on a chair and drops a sheet of paper. As it floats to the ground, another child tries to catch it. To make it harder, require the catcher to use only her thumb and first finger.

Fun with Pennies

1. Put a secret number of pennies into your closed fist. Have your kids guess whether there is an odd or even number of pennies.

2. See if your child can balance a penny on each of her fingertips. Now see if she can transfer them to the other hand by putting one hand on the other (finger-to-finger) and flipping her hands over.

3. Give each child an equal number of pennies. The first player tosses a penny against a wall and leaves it where it lands. Then each player in  turn bounces a penny off of the wall, trying to make it land so that it touches another penny. If it does, he picks up and keeps both pennies. If not, he leaves it and the game continues.

4. The kids can take turns tossing a penny and guessing whether it will land heads up or tails up. The first one to guess correctly ten times wins!

6 Games to Play with (Very) Old Magazines

1. Waiting Room Race: Each child takes two old magazines and puts them on the floor. At "Go!" the kids begin to make their way across the room by stepping on the first magazine, then the second, then moving the first magazine forward for the third step. If a child steps off a magazine, he goes back to the start.

2. Paper Puzzle: Rip out a colorful page from a very old magazine. Tear it into pieces and let your child put it back together like a puzzle.

3. Peephole: Tear a coin-size hole in a plain piece of paper (beg one from the receptionist) and place it on top of a magazine photo. Can anyone guess what the photo is, based on the visible piece?

4. Once Upon a Time: Hold up a photo in a magazine for everyone to see. Begin making up a story about the picture and have each child add a sentence.

5. Scavenger Hunt: Everyone turn to a page and look for things beginning with the letter *S*. (Get creative: A lemon can be *sour*.)

6. Balancing Act: Try to walk across the waiting room and back balancing a magazine on your head.

Cat and Mouse

Any large piece of furniture can be the hunting grounds: A couch or coffee table works well. Two children are blindfolded (or trusted to keep their eyes closed) and placed at opposite ends of the table or sofa. One is the cat and the other is the mouse. Keeping their hands on the furniture at all times, the cat tries to catch the mouse and the mouse tries to avoid the cat—each without being able to see where the other is. After the cat has successfully hunted down the mouse, they can trade places.

My Robot

Two kids can take
turns being Robot
and Robot's
Owner. The robot has
three imaginary buttons on his
back: In the middle of his back is
a Go Forward button; on his
right shoulder is a Turn Right
button; on his left shoulder is a
Turn Left button. The robot
closes his eyes and the owner
presses a button (and keeps
pressing it as long as he wants
the robot to move). If no button
is being pushed, the robot stops.

Hide the Man

This version of hide-and-seek, which requires less space than the traditional game and makes it unlikely that you will inadvertently lose your child, is perfect for a waiting room.

Find a two-sided ad in a magazine— or any page in a very old magazine—

Tip: If your child is anxious when waiting for his dentist's or doctor's appointment, activities like Alphaback (page 214) or Head Massage (page 19) serve not only to redirect behavior toward a quiet activity but also provide a soothing and calming distraction. Games like these are better choices for nervous little patients than more active ones.

with a picture of a man, and tear out his head. Take turns hiding the picture of the man's head while the others have their eyes closed. Whoever finds the man hides him next! (The hider can help the seekers by saying "Warmer!" and "Colder!" the closer and farther away the seekers get to the man.)

Active Waiting in the Waiting Room

If the waiting room is relatively large and your young child refuses to sit still to do *anything* and the nurses and receptionists are laid-back (a lot of ifs), try these games:

- Use shoes as baskets and rolled up socks as balls for a little basketball action.

- Make two sock balls and throw them back and forth to each other at the same time.

- Try throwing and catching sock balls with the wrong hand.

- Have the child take off his socks and roll them into a ball, then use a rolled-up magazine as a bat.

doctor's office games

O nce
you've
moved
from the waiting
room to the exam

room, you feel as if you're making
progress. Trouble is, now you're
waiting in a much tinier room with a
child who is very unhappy because
he is wearing only underwear and
socks and is worried that he will be
getting a shot. The waiting game has
become a bit more anxiety-ridden.

But there are a number of games
you can play in the doctor's office

that will keep his mind off the impending exam and make the experience as pleasant as possible. Any props mentioned  (cotton balls, tongue depressors, paper cups) should be readily available. Most doctors don't mind being down a few disposable gloves if it means encountering a giggling patient rather than a howling one.

Sock 'Em

Thankfully, most doctors' offices come equipped with all sorts of interesting things that can be turned into toys—like paper cups. (Look for a dispenser next to the sink.) Children can take turns stacking the cups and then tossing a rolled-up pair of socks to knock them over. (This is a great game if you have only one child with you, because she can be the cup stacker *and* the sock tosser!)

Fun with Pennies in the Exam Room

1. Put a magazine on the floor and then place a penny on it. You and your child can take turns trying to knock the penny off by throwing a ball of socks at it. The one who finally knocks it off is the winner.

2. Hide a penny in the room and see if your child can find it.

3. Have your child hold a penny above his head, and try to drop it into one of his shoes.

Body Double

Have your child lie
down on the
examination
table and
outline him or her
on the disposable
paper with a pen or
marker. Then let your child fill in
the details: face, hair, clothes,
shoes. When you are done, just
pull and tear off the used paper.

Push-Pull

Have two kids squat down, facing each other, and grab each other's arms. They must push and pull on each other but try not to let the other one tip over.

Shake, Rattle, and Guess

Put several coins, paper clips, mints, or any other small items you have on hand into a paper cup. Fold the top over and let your child shake it, trying to guess just by listening to the sound how many items are in the cup. If he guesses right, he can try to fool you!

Note: This game can be played anywhere you have access to something that will hold a number of small items without allowing anyone to see them—try a paper bag, small box, or even a sock!

5 Things to Do with Cotton Balls and a Wristwatch

It helps to have a second hand for these games (if you don't, you can always count aloud). Time how fast or how long kids can:

1. Balance a cotton ball on a tongue depressor and walk from one end of the exam room to the other without dropping it.

2. Move cotton balls stuffed into a paper cup into an empty cup, one by one, using only two tongue depressors (as you'd use salad tongs).

3. Balance a cotton ball on their nose.

4. Jump across the room holding a cotton ball between their knees (without dropping it).

5. Walk in and out of a row of cotton balls: Line up cotton balls on the ground about every 2 feet. Tuck a long length of toilet paper into the back waistband of your child's pants. Walk in and out without allowing the toilet paper tail to touch any of the cotton balls.

Test Your Cents of Hearing

Divide the pennies in your wallet into two piles by date: One pile should contain pennies that are dated 1982 and before; the other pile should contain pennies that are dated 1983 and after.

Tell your child to close her eyes and hand her a penny from one of the piles. Have her drop it onto the hard floor. After a number of penny drops, she should be able to tell the two piles of pennies apart based upon sound: The newer pennies contain zinc as well as copper and make a duller sound when they hit the floor.

Handbag Memories

Dump out the contents of your purse. Let the kids look at everything for a minute or two, then put all of the items back. The kids can take turns naming the items they saw. As soon as someone is stumped, the other one wins!

8 Crazy Things to Do with Disposable Gloves

Help yourselves to a couple of the disposable gloves that doctors use for exams. Blow them up like balloons, secure the ends, and . . .

1. Give your child two and have him try to use them in place of his hands.

2. Draw faces on them (with the fingers acting as crazy hair) and do a puppet show.

3. See who can throw one the farthest.

4. See if your child can keep one up in the air by tapping it with a pencil as she walks across the room and back.

5. Ask your child to try to keep two up in the air while his feet stay frozen in place.

6. Play Keep Away.

7. Challenge two kids to walk across the room with one glove wedged between them.

8. Have two kids stand back-to-back with one glove between them and try to turn to the front, keeping it in place without using their hands.

6 Ways to Play with Shoelaces

1. Remove someone's shoelace and use it as a ruler to measure the office: Is it 10 shoelaces long and 8 laces wide? How long is the examination table? How high off the ground?

2. Lay a shoelace on the ground as a balance beam. Kids can attempt jumps and balancing on one leg— but if they fall off the beam, their turn is over!

3. Arrange the shoelaces on the ground to create numbers or letters. Who can guess correctly?

4. Guess what objects in the room are fatter and which are thinner, then wrap a shoelace around each to determine who guessed correctly.

5. Tie a tongue depressor to the end of a shoelace and try to land it exactly on top of another tongue depressor you've placed on the floor.

6. Stretch out two shoelaces on the floor parallel to one another, but several feet apart. Can anyone jump from one to the other? Move them farther apart and try again.

Play Doctor

As you wait for the doctor to come into the exam room, calm the jitters with a little role reversal. Tell your child that *she* can be the doctor.

- Show her how to take a pulse: Press two fingers against the side of the neck or inside the wrist, count the beats for 15 seconds, then multiply by 4. Take a pulse again after doing jumping jacks.

- Have your child sit and cross her legs. Tap her gently just below her kneecap. When you hit the right spot, her leg will jump! Now she can play doctor and check your reflexes.

Carnival Game

Place a series a paper cups on the floor and give your child a handful of pennies to try to toss into the cups for varying numbers of points, the farthest away being worth the most points.

Guess What?

Here are some guessing games you can play while you wait for the doctor. Ask your child to:

- Guess how many people you'll see if you peek into the hallway.

- Guess how many tongue depressors you need to place end-to-end to span the length of the exam table.

- Guess how high he will have to count before he hears a phone ring, or a baby making noise, or a doctor talking.

- Guess how much her shoe weighs (on the baby scale).

- Guess how many paper cups she can stack (right side up, on top of, upside down, etc.).

- Guess how long he can balance a cotton ball on the end of a tongue depressor— while marching in place.

My Secret

Think of a secret category and count how many items in that category you see. Tell your child, "I see three," and let her guess three of what. It could be three posters on the wall, three stethoscopes, three stools . . . If she guesses right, it's her turn to think of a category.

Stick Drop

Each child can take turns dropping a handful of tongue depressors from chest height into a paper cup placed on the floor. The one who gets the most tongue depressors in after three turns wins!

Two Eyes Are Better Than One

Ever wonder why you
need two eyes? Try
catching a pair of
rolled-up socks
with one eye closed.
Hard, huh? Now hold a pencil or
pen in each hand, close one eye,
and try to make the points touch
in front of you. Challenge the
kids to keep trying to see if they
could learn to compensate for
the closed eye.

Juggling

During that seemingly endless wait between the nurse's departure (after jotting down your child's height and weight) and the appearance of your pediatrician, your child can try juggling three or four of these items that you might find in the exam room or might have with you:

- cotton balls

- tissues

- wadded-up paper cups

- tongue depressors

- balled-up socks

4 Games to Play with Your Toes

What better time to invent games to play with your toes than when your kids are sitting barefoot waiting for the doctor to appear?

1. Challenge your child to pick up a pencil with his toes and then write his name.

2. Draw a face on the bottom of each big toe, and the kids can put on a puppet show.

3. See how long your kids can keep perfectly still while you tickle the bottoms of their toes with a tissue.

4. See if the kids can untie their shoes using only their toes.

grocery store games

We might have named this section "Mission: Impossible." Nearly every mom has a story of abandoning a half-full grocery cart in Aisle 7 and marching out of the store with a howling child under each arm. Executing a successful grocery store mission is definitely something to brag about at the next Moms' Club meeting.

Common sense dictates that you shop with a child who is well rested and that you hit

the store when it's least likely to be crowded. An early-morning trip works well from both of these standpoints. Avoid shift change time—often mid-afternoon—as that might mean fewer registers are open.

The grocery store games that follow range from educational (teaching kids about unit pricing) to silly (Toilet Paper Toss), but all serve to keep kids content in or near the cart as you work your way up and down the aisles. Good luck!

Toilet Paper Toss

A personal favorite, this game also works with paper towels, napkins, or anything soft and unbreakable. Park your grocery cart as far away from the toilet paper as possible, and position your kids so that they're evenly spaced between the cart and the toilet paper. Pick up the rolls one at a time and begin tossing them to the person closest to you, who tosses them to the person next to her, and so on, until the last person slam-dunks into the cart. Start the second roll moving down the line as soon as possible to make the game crazier. You'll find that witnesses to this game will be amused, not annoyed.

6 Ways to Avoid Checkout Line Meltdown

1. Take turns finding things that begin with the letters of the alphabet in order: aisle, baby, cart . . .

2. Have your child close her eyes and put out her hand. Place something in her hand and then quickly put it back before she opens her eyes. She must guess what she was holding.

3. Tell your child to pretend to hide somewhere close by and you will try to guess where he is hiding. He can tell you if you are getting warmer or colder.

4. Engage your cart-bound child in a visual scavenger hunt using magazine covers: "Can you find a blue letter *M*?" "Can you find a man riding a horse?" "Can you find a poodle?"

5. As a variation on the game above, take turns naming things you can see, adding on the previously mentioned items.

Parent: "I see a picture of a lady in a red dress."

Child: "I see a picture of a lady in a red dress and a package of purple gum."

Parent: "I see a picture of a lady in a red dress and a package of purple gum and the number 12 on a sign . . ."

6. Ask your child to guess how many things he thinks you bought at the store. Then, as the items are scanned, he can count them. An older child who guesses 39 can count backwards from 39 to see if he was right.

TIP: When you first get to the store, grab a six- or eight-pack of paper towels and a comic book. Your child can sit in the cart on top of the paper towels (rather than the metal grating) and leaf through the comic book.

Runaway Cart

Younger kids love this game that combines a bit of suspense with the reassurance of a predictable rescue.

With your little one sitting in the front seat of the cart, gently push the cart, let go, and squeal, "Oh no! My darling's getting away from me!" Run a few steps toward the cart and grab it, saving your little guy. (An added bonus of this game is that you keep moving right along, adding items to the cart as you do.)

Putting Your Big Kids to Good Use

Older kids may not throw tantrums (or they may), but they can still make a trip to the supermarket less than pleasant if they decide to. Here are some ideas for keeping them happily entertained (and helping out in the bargain!):

- Give them a shopping basket and your coupons and ask them to find the coupon items. If you're feeling especially generous, tell them they can have half of the money you save.

- Let them select one item that they've never tried before.

grocery store games

- Give them a calculator and say, "Please get me $5 worth of canned cat food" or "Please pick out $8 worth of snacks."

- Ask them to get all of the food necessary to make tacos, spaghetti and meatballs, or whatever you have planned for dinner. Let them think through all that will be needed to make the meal.

- Teach them how unit pricing works and send them off to find ten cans of the least expensive dog food or three boxes of the least expensive tissues.

- Older kids and the produce
  section are a great combination.
  They can pick
  through the
  green beans to
  find the best
  ones, and they
  can weigh
  potatoes and
  tomatoes on the
  hanging scales.

Cart and Driver

So your little fellow wants to push the cart, eh? Tell him he can—as long as he doesn't lose the ten points you'll give him to start. He loses one point if he bumps something and five points if he bumps someone. He can earn back points: one point for every time he stops his cart to let someone else go first. If he ends up with ten points or more when you reach the checkout, he can pick out a treat.

Supermarket Showdown

Challenge your older kids to a race (though they must walk through the store, not run). As you enter the store, get them each a handheld basket. Let them take turns picking items off your grocery list that

TIP: When it is time to pay for the groceries, put your child in charge. It's never too early to begin teaching life skills. He can count out the cash and try to figure out how much change he'll get back; he can slide your debit card and press the correct buttons; or he can write out a check and just leave the signature line blank.

they want to get (for a total of five or so items). Then send them off in search of their items. Whoever returns to you first with all of the correct items wins a point. You can send them off again with five new items to find. The loser has to take all the groceries from the car into the house.

What Costs More

Older kids can play a guessing game with the items on your list that will teach them about unit pricing and the relative cost of things. Have them guess, for instance, whether a pound of chicken or a pound of breakfast cereal costs more. Then send them in search of both items with instructions to remember the unit price of each to see who was right!

Driver's Ed. 101

If your child wants to push the cart but is too little to do so alone, you can have him hold the cart as if he were pushing, but put his feet on the lower part of the cart. From behind, you wrap your arms around him, put your hands next to his, and drive—but listen to his instructions. He tells you when to stop, go, turn left, and turn right.

Hide-and-Seek

Find something interesting when you first walk into the store and tuck it on a shelf where it doesn't belong (put a stuffed dog in the pet food area or Happy Face paper plates among the cookies, for example). As soon as your child starts to get fussy, say, "Let's check to see if anyone discovered our secret!" It depends on how diligent the store employees are—you may find your item gone the first time you check or it

may still be there two days later! (An older child can choose an item, show it to you, then hide it by himself. You try to find it as you work your way through the store.)

TIP: Kids love the new grocery carts that look like little cars. If you take two children with you on a shopping trip, however, there may be some loud discussions regarding who will be the driver and who will be the passenger. Assign one to drive down the odd-numbered aisles and the other the even-numbered ones. (You will find they learn their odds and evens very quickly this way.)

Finders Keepers

This will speed up your grocery shopping! Every time you turn down a different aisle, tell your kids what you're looking for: applesauce, chocolate chips, Cheerios . . . The first one to spot an item on your list gets one point. You can award a pack of gum or stickers to the one who is first to accumulate the winning number of points: his or her age multiplied by three.

hairdresser games

Hair salons do not necessarily welcome waiting children (and certainly don't want them playing active games), but sometimes you must arrive with a child or two in tow. If you do, check out the good ideas in the Waiting Room or Anywhere sections of the book. (This is also a good time to bring along some quiet activities. See Bag of Tricks, page 310). In addition, there are some nifty hair salon items that can be used for child's play (with the permission of the salon owner, of course).

7 Ways to Keep Your Child Occupied While You Get a Trim

1. While you're getting your hair washed, your child can write you a message using her index finger in the palm of your hand, one letter at a time. If she's not reading and writing yet, she can put something in your hand that you must try to identify.

2. Ask the stylist for a few sheets of the foil used for highlighting. These can be turned into wonderfully unique sculptures. Think Calder or Moore!

3. Ask if your daughter can sit in a free stylist's chair to look in the mirror and do her own hair or her sister's using the brushes, combs, and various clips at hand. Show her how to turn around and use a hand mirror to see the back of her head in the larger mirror.

4. Velcro rollers are like round, squishy LEGOS—kids can stick them together to make interesting shapes. If your salon is kid-friendly, they might let your child play with the rollers for a little while.

hairdresser games

5. Kids love the swatches stylists use to help clients choose a hair color. Some salons have them hanging on a large chart that can be taken down and played with gently.

6. Kids love to sit under the dryers (which means they can't hear the hair salon gossip).

7. And, if utterly desperate: The stylists' chairs that twirl around and go up and down are a blast to play with, though most salons discourage it. A last resort.

TIP: Always call the hair salon as you are ready to leave for your scheduled appointment to ask if the hairdresser is running on time. If you explain that you will be bringing children with you, the salon is more likely to provide you with accurate information.

3 Fun Things to Do with Hairdo Books

Most salons (even barbershops) have magazines, books, or posters featuring various hairstyle possibilities. These are fun to look at in themselves, but here are some amusing games to play with them.

1. Ask your child to name any person he knows well. Now have him flip through the pages of the hairstyles books or magazines to choose a new hairdo for his best friend or relative. Guaranteed giggles!

TIP: If you are mid-cut and your little one is acting up, offer $5 or so to one of the available stylists to paint her (or his!) fingernails or toenails.

2. Ask your child to pick a person from the book or magazine (the more unusual the hairstyle the better!) and to make up identifying details about her—her name, what she does, where she lives, her favorite activities, what pets she has, her favorite food . . .

3. Have your child close her eyes, open the book or magazine, and point. Tell her that the person she chose will be her future husband! She can try again and blindly choose her new best friend, next substitute teacher—whatever pops into your mind. Then it's her turn to close her eyes, flip through the pages, and point to some people who may be in *your* future: your new boss, next aerobics instructor, doctor . . .

Hairdresser's Helper

Waiting kids can also be put to work. Ask if they can help by sweeping up hair, organizing the magazines or toys, or folding towels.

TIP: One hairdresser swears the secret to getting very young kids to wait patiently while their own hair is being cut is to put a comb in each of their hands. This preoccupies them and prevents them from putting their hands in the way of the cut. (For whatever reason, they tend not to try combing their hair with the combs! Go figure.)

standing-in-line games

Whether it's 10 minutes at the post office or bank or 45 minutes at Disneyland or the Department of Motor Vehicles, waiting in line with kids poses a challenge for even the most playful parents. Here are some ideas to complement your own repertoire.

Alphaback

Can you read what someone is "writing" on your back? Take turns using a fingertip to outline letters on each other's back. For younger children, write individual letters or numbers or draw pictures. Added bonus: It feels great!

Tongue Twisters

Remember these from childhood? Can you say each one three times—fast?

- Unique New York

- Selfish shellfish

- Knapsack straps

- Black bug's blood

- We surely shall see the sun shine soon.

- Shredded Swiss cheese

- Six sticky sucker sticks

- Sam's shop stocks short spotted socks.

- Mrs. Smith's Fish Sauce Shop

And, for those with six-year-old boys:

- One smart fellow, he felt smart.

Count on It

As you wait in line, predict how high you will have to count before:

- someone laughs

- the person in front of you takes a step

- someone smiles at you

- a door closes

- someone says, "Thank you."

- someone wearing a red shirt joins the line

Slaphappy

This addictive little game has entertained kids of preschool age and older for generations. Have one person (the slapper) put her hands out in front of her, palms up. The other player puts his hands out, palms down, hovering a few inches directly above hers. At any time, the slapper can flip her hands up and over to try to hit the back of her opponent's hands. When she does, it's his turn to be the slapper.

Air Writing

Pretending that they are holding large pieces of chalk, kids can take turns writing giant words in the air for the others to decipher.

A variation: One child can stand behind another. The player in back can use the other's arm to write words. The player in front must guess what the words are.

TIP: Ask your child to mentally compose a short note to a friend or grandparent. When you get to the teller, buy a prestamped postcard. Your child can either tell you the note or quickly write it out himself. Address it and drop it in the slot.

Trash Can Ball

Crumple up several blank deposit slips or a brochure and, from your place in line, ask your child to throw the ball into the nearest trash can. She earns more points per basket as you move up in line and farther away from the trash can.

Rock, Paper, Scissors

At "Rock, paper, scissors, shoot!" two children bring their right hands from behind their backs to reveal their fingers in one of three positions: a fist (representing a rock), flat (paper), or with the index and middle fingers held apart like a pair of scissors.

The critical thing is that they shoot simultaneously so that no one has a tactical advantage.

The winner of a given round is determined this way: Rock crushes scissors, paper covers rock, and scissors cuts paper. The players assess their hand positions and determine a winner.

(Your kids may want to morph this game and add their own element with its particular strengths and weaknesses.)

Odds and Evens

Odds and Evens is played much like Rock, Paper, Scissors, except that each player yells "Odds!" or "Evens!" and then both simultaneously shoot a certain number of fingers. Whoever guesses correctly wins a point.

A variation: Players shoot a chosen number of fingers at the same time that they guess the total number that will be shot by the two players combined. If no one guesses correctly, it's a draw. If someone does guess the correct number, she wins the round!

The Best Guess

Play these guessing games as you wait in line:

- Guess what the next person who gets in line will look like.

- Guess whether any other kids will come into the post office while you're there.

- Guess exactly what the person at the counter will say to you when you approach.

- Guess whether or not the person behind you in line will smile at you if you turn around.

Would You Rather . . .

Would You Rather . . . is one of those strange games that kids love to play and adults don't quite understand (not a problem as long as you have at least two kids with you). One child starts by asking the other, "Would you rather . . ." and offering two different but equally appealing or unappealing options (win the lottery or meet a magic genie; be lost in the woods overnight or hear noises in the attic when you're home alone). The game does not produce a winner or loser, just lots of interesting discussions.

Fun, Initially

Players take turns asking questions that the others must answer in two words beginning with his or her initials. So Sam Chase's favorite food could be Swiss cheese and Beth Gifford's most prized possession might be her baseball glove. If a player takes longer than five seconds to answer or gives an incorrect answer (like naming a television show rather than the requested movie title), he's out!

outside games

At some point, every parent finds herself waiting outside with the kids. This can be tricky because the same children who cling to you in the house and refuse to go upstairs alone seem more than willing to explore dark alleyways, busy intersections, or something that resembles quicksand.

There are games in this section for large open spaces that allow for running and chasing, games for one child or a group, and quieter games that keep children near you when safety is an issue.

For more ideas, see page 280.

Hop Off

In this giggle-inducing way to use up time and excess energy, the kids face each other and begin hopping forward on one foot. The goal of each child is to cause another to lose his balance—resulting in both feet on the ground—without any physical contact whatsoever. (Fake tickling works well!)

High Tide

This game can be played with as few as two children or as many as a dozen (more kids do make it more fun). One child (or group of children) is the wave, the other is the shell collector. The children stand some distance apart, and an object (the shell) is placed between them. At "Go!" the shell collector tries to grab the shell and take it back to her original spot, while the wave tries to tag the shell collector before she's able to get back.

TIP: On a blustery fall day, the kids can try to catch leaves as they're blown out of the trees. Offer a dime for every leaf they catch out of the air (chances are you won't have to give out too many dimes—it's tough.)

Twists on Tag

The classic game of tag has myriad incarnations—here are a few of the most fun.

Hat Tag

In this crazier version of tag, the player who is it chases only the person wearing the hat (any available hat). The player wearing the hat attempts to give it away before he is tagged. When a player is touched by the person with the hat, the player must take the hat and wear it until he has managed to tag someone else and pass the hat along.

TIP: After a snowfall, stomp down a wagon wheel pattern in the snow and play tag, staying within the spokes.

Safety Tag

The players agree to designate a certain category of thing as "safety." (For example it can be anything that is made of wood, or anything that's the color red, etc.) Whenever kids are close to being tagged, they can try to touch an appropriate item and be "safe." (Players can decide to limit the number of times and for how long the safety can be used.)

Shadow Tag

In this version of tag, instead of tagging another player, the player who is it must step on the shadow of another player and call out that person's name. Then the

person whose shadow was caught becomes the new it.

Got Your Tail!

Before herding the gang outside, stop by the restrooms and get everyone a toilet paper tail. (Gently tuck a piece of toilet paper into everyone's back pocket. It should be just long enough to brush the ground.) Decide who will be it. Rather than tagging people, the person who's it tries to pull off the other players' tails.

Once someone's tail is pulled off, he joins the one who's it and tries to pull off others' tails.

Cutoff Tag

If the player who is it is chasing someone, another player can run between them, and the one who's it must begin pursuing that other player. Older children can keep their younger siblings from getting tagged too soon with this variation.

Freeze Tag

An oldie but goodie: Anyone who is tagged by the person who is it must freeze in place until touched (unfrozen) by another player.

Backpack Tag

This game is good for kids who are on their way home from school. The child who is it covers her ears as the others count off. As soon as each child has a number, they scatter and put their backpacks at their feet.

(If you don't have backpacks, use a sweater or even a twig to mark your place.) The person who is it stands on the edge of the group and calls out two numbers. The players who have those two numbers dash to each other's backpacks as the player who is it tries to get to one of the backpacks first. If she does, the player whom she outran becomes it. If she doesn't, she calls out two different numbers.

Chain Gang Tag

As soon as someone is tagged, she grabs the hand of the player who is it and they pursue other players together. Every time a player is tagged, he joins the chain. The players at both ends of the chain can tag.

The Real Feel

Have your child close her eyes
(or blindfold her). Turn her around
several times, then walk her to
a tree, rock, patch of moss, or a
distinctive piece of ground. Have
her run her fingers over it until she
thinks she can identify it. Walk her
back to her starting point and turn
her around several more times to
make the guessing harder. When
her eyes are open, can she find the
object she touched?

Making a Masterpiece

Children can create a masterpiece with the ground as their canvas using the natural materials at hand: leaves, moss, sticks, pinecones, flowers, stones, shells, etc. Younger children can dash around collecting things, and then together you can create the work of art.

Sounds All Around

Give the kids five minutes to listen for all of the different sounds they can hear (a raindrop, a woodpecker, the wind, a truck in the distance). Then gather  them together and have them take turns imitating a sound. If a child can't come up with a sound, she's out, and the game continues until there's a winner.

What Can You Remember?

Have the kids look carefully all around them for a minute. Then tell them to close their eyes while you ask them questions to test their memory: What color was the restaurant sign? What is the shape of the leaves of the nearest tree? How many red cars are in the parking lot? Is there a sign about pets nearby?

Invent-a-Cise

Tell the kids they have to invent a new kind of exercise (like some sort of variation on jumping jacks or push-ups). Give them a few minutes to think, then they can try them out and teach each other.

On Base

Everyone stands in a large circle and puts a backpack or jacket or an X made of twigs at their feet to mark their spot. One child stands in the middle of the circle. When she says "Go!" each child runs to the next space while she tries to beat one of them there. If she succeeds, she trades places with the one she beat.

Pebble Jacks

Your kids can play jacks, but
with pebbles! Each player
selects one pebble for tossing
in the air and then the players
put a dozen or so pebbles in a
pile in the middle of the group.
As in traditional jacks, a child
tosses a pebble up in the air
and picks one up from the pile
with the same hand, then
catches her tossed pebble. Her
turn continues until she misses.
When the pile is gone, whoever
has the most pebbles wins!

Stick It

A parent finds a blunt stick, shows the kids what it looks like, and then hides it within an agreed upon area (while the kids close their eyes). Everyone then decides what will serve as home base (a tree, for example). At "Go!" the players rush around looking for the stick. Whoever finds it chases the others, trying to tag them with the stick before they reach home base. He gets one point for each person he tags. A parent hides the stick again as the game continues.

Step Right Up

Because luck determines the winner of this game, younger kids are not at a disadvantage. Have the kids sit on the bottom of a set of steps. The goal is to be the first one to reach the top step. The parent (or an older child) switches a pebble from one hand to the other, then asks the first player to guess which hand it's in. If he guesses correctly, he moves up a step. Then the parent repeats the pebble switching and asks the second player to guess. The game continues until someone reaches the top step!

Shoe Toss

Have each child loosen the shoe on one foot and remove the heel so that the shoe is dangling on the toes. At the count of three, everyone kicks off his or her shoe and sees whose goes the farthest. Not all that intellectually stimulating, but fun nonetheless.

Twig Match

Have the kids collect a bunch of twigs and bring them to you. Now break each twig in half, putting one set of halves in one pile and one set in another pile. How quickly can the kids match the twig halves? You can time them and offer a prize if they do it in under a certain number of minutes.

Who Am I?

Standing behind her, hold
an object above your child's
head (a leaf, a rock, a
mushroom, a pinecone) for
another child to see. The
child under the object asks
the other one, "Who am I?"
followed by a series of yes
or no questions like "Am I
alive?" or "Am I soft?" or
"Do I change colors?" She
asks questions until she
guesses correctly.

Blind Man Walking

One child (the Blind Man) stands in the middle of the group with his eyes closed. The other children take four giant steps away from him and freeze in place. The Blind Man spins around several times and then begins walking with arms outstretched (and eyes still closed). As he approaches the kids, flailing his arms to try to touch them, they can bend, swerve, and duck to avoid being caught but must keep at least one foot frozen in place. To be replaced, the Blind Man must not only tag another child but also identify him.

Nature Bingo

Send the kids off on an adventure (with the understanding that they must always be able to see you) in search of something:

- absolutely straight

- squishy

- shaped like a heart

- red

- broken or cracked

- prickly

- that makes a noise

- that makes them think of you

- round

- that has been chewed

- that could tickle someone

- _____ (Add your own category.)

A variation: Quickly gather a dozen or so easy-to-find items nearby like a rock, leaf, pinecone, seashell, or berry. Have the kids close their eyes as you lay them out on the ground. When you are ready, have them open their eyes and examine the items on display for ten seconds. They must commit the items to memory and then run around in search of things to create the very same display. The first one to do that wins!

Pebbles

This game is especially good for just two children. Have them collect a small pile of pebbles and sit facing each other. One begins the game by passing a pebble from one hand to the other, trying to make it difficult for the other player to keep track of which hand it is in. When the player holding the pebble is ready, he holds out both fists and the other player must guess which hand the pebble is in. If the guesser is correct, she keeps the pebble and it is her turn to pick another pebble from the pile and pass it from hand to hand. When the pile is gone, the player with the most pebbles wins!

bus stop games

I f you add it up, you'll discover that kids spend quite a bit of time waiting at the bus stop. Why not suggest ways to make the time pass pleasantly? Parents often accompany their kids to the bus stop for the first week or so of school. This is a perfect time to introduce some game concepts.

Bus Stop Games differ from those in the Outside Games chapter in a few significant ways. Children waiting for a bus are standing close to the street in a

residential area. They may be unsupervised. Play needs to be contained and games must not be too distracting—kids caught up in a game of tag, for instance, might run into the road while being chased. The games described in this section consider safety first.

In addition, kids are dressed for school with backpacks on, rather than for outdoor play, so rough-and-tumble games should be discouraged. And the amount of time they have for play is limited—hopefully, less than ten minutes or so each morning. The games that follow take these factors into account while still providing kids with a great start to the day!

Simon Does

In the traditional Simon Says game, Simon gives orders which must be followed only when preceded with "Simon Says." In this newer version, Simon's *actions* must be imitated, unless he puts his hands on his knees, in which case the players clap instead. For older kids, Simon can add one more action for which a clap must be substituted. Another way to play this game is to instruct players to do what Simon does, not what he says. So if Simon says, "Stand!" but he sits, everyone must sit!

Knot Happening

All the kids at the bus stop but one hold hands in a circle. With the single child covering his or her eyes, the circle of kids tangle themselves into a knot by stepping over each other's hands. The one outside the circle must untangle the group by telling them what to do. No cheating! The kids can't let go of each other's hands!

Who's Got It?

One child stands in the center of a tight circle. The other children begin passing something (anything about the size of a tennis ball) behind their backs. They are trying to fool the child in the center, who must point to the child who is holding the object at any given moment. Fake-outs are encouraged!

Snake Tag

This is a bus stop–friendly version of tag because the kids are not dashing in all directions. Kids divide themselves into two teams and line up one behind another. Each child puts her arms on the waist of the person in front of her, creating two human snakes. The head of one snake tries to grab the tail of the other. If the tail is caught, he drops out and the person in front of him becomes the new tail. Play continues until one snake is only one kid long.

Freeze Frame

One child stands with his back to the others, who are about 15 feet behind him. When he says "Go!" the kids quietly make their way toward him, ready to freeze if he turns and looks. At any time, he can twirl around and try to catch someone moving. If he does, that person is out! If someone manages to touch him without being seen in motion, they trade places.

Blind Man in the Middle

One child who is it closes his eyes (or pulls his hat over his eyes) and holds out a long stick. The other children hold hands and circle around him. When the person who is it hits the ground three times with the stick, everyone freezes in place. He points the stick at someone and

commands, "Speak like
a _____ (cow, lion, dog)."
The chosen player does
as he is told, trying to
disguise his voice. If the
person who is it guesses
who spoke, that player
takes his place. If not,
the game continues.

Pebble Toss

In Mexico, this traditional game is played with beans rather than pebbles.

Draw a circle in the dirt about the size of a dinner plate. Each child picks up ten pebbles and stands behind a stick placed several feet away. One by one, every player tosses his pebbles toward the circle. He picks up the ones that land within the circle, places them on the back of his hand, tosses them up, and tries to catch as many in his palm as he can. After everyone has had a turn, whoever has the most pebbles in his hand wins!

airplane
games

Because most airplane trips are planned well in advance, you'll have plenty of time to think about what you can do so that the kids enjoy the trip as much as the arrival at their final destination. But when all the toys, snacks, books, and art supplies you thoughtfully brought along lose their appeal, try these activities. (And for a few more thoughts on plane travel with kids, see page 325.)

Barf Bag Fun

Thankfully, most air
sickness bags are not
used for their intended
purpose, but they can
be used to amuse kids.

1. Make a puppet: Draw a face on
the side of the bag and poke a hole
for a finger nose.

2. Put something inside the bag
and let your child shake it to try
to figure out what it is.

3. Put lots of little somethings
(like coins) in the bag and have your
child guess how many there are
by shaking the bag. Then she can
count them to see if she was right.

4. Draw a monster face on the bag, blow into it, then twist the top of the bag (like a tuft of hair). Set it on the tray and try to knock it off by throwing wadded up pieces of paper at it.

5. Take the same monster bag and see how long you can balance it on top of a rolled-up magazine or catalog (look in the seat pocket).

6. Draw an upside-down monster face on the bag. Blow into it and twist the bag closed. Tuck the twisted end between two of your fingers and let your child try to punch the monster to the floor.

7. Tear off the bottom so the bag becomes a tube. Now ask your child to decorate it and then put it on like a piece of clothing (a sleeve or pant leg). Borrow bags from those around you to create an entire outfit.

8. Draw a sleeping face on the bag. Stuff an airplane pillow inside, then swaddle your paper bag baby in an airplane blanket. Instant baby doll!

TIP: Start your trip off on the right foot at the check-in line. One parent can wait in line while the other parent stays nearby with the kids, letting them move around more freely. As soon as the parent on line reaches the counter, everyone can join up.

Tissue Toss

Turn the air nozzle on and point it toward you. If you take a piece of tissue and let it go a few inches from the air source, where will it land? Will it always land in the same place?

Silly Games with the Sky Mall Catalog

- Tell the kids to pretend they are doing their holiday shopping from the catalog. With an unlimited budget, what would they buy for their family and friends?

- Take turns closing your eyes, flipping the pages, and pointing: That's what you're getting for your birthday! Do you want to keep it or trade it for the next item that you will point to after flipping the pages with your eyes closed? (Even if you decide to keep your first item, you have to keep playing to see what you *would* have gotten if you had traded.)

- Challenge each other to a catalog scavenger hunt: Find a dog, a boy, a shoe, a tool, a chair, a car, and a summer toy.

TIP: As you board, ask the flight attendant if the airline supplies a kid's activity pack. It won't entertain him for too long, but ten minutes of scribbling in a new coloring book gets you ten minutes closer to your destination.

Guessing Games to Play on the Airplane

With their eyes closed, can the kids guess:

• how many people are seated in the rows behind them?

• how many rows away is an exit row?

• whether there are any rows in front of them that have two empty seats?

• if they turn around, will they see anyone behind them standing up?

- whether anyone in the row behind them is listening to music (wearing headphones)?

- whether the seat belt light is still on?

- if more people on the plane have their window shades open or closed?

- whether the plane is flying above or below the clouds?

TIP: When the airline personnel offer early boarding for parents with young children, have one parent board with all of the kiddie paraphernalia to be sure that there is enough space in the overhead bins to accommodate your stuff. The other parent can stay near the gate and let the kids run around until the very last minute.

Map Mind-Benders

Most airplane seat pockets contain a map showing the various routes that particular airline flies. As soon as the kids have located theirs, you can play map games.

• Before they look at the maps, have your kids guess what states you will be flying over as you travel from your departure city to your destination city.

• Quiz the kids on time zones: If it is 2:30 P.M. in Denver, what time is it in Baltimore?

- Have the kids close their eyes, then ask them to guess which trip would be longer: New York City to Miami or New York City to Dallas (as an example)? The kids can take turns quizzing each other about hypothetical trips.

- See if the kids can point out all the states they've visited.

- Can the kids show you where various relatives live?

- Quiz the kids on state capitals.

Card Quiz

Let your kids read the information on the emergency card (tucked in the seat pocket in front of them). When they're done, tell them to put it where they can't see it. Now make up a quiz based on the information on the card. The child who answers the most questions correctly may change seats with anyone in your group!

while-mom-is-busy games

There are some times when your child is waiting, but you aren't; you are otherwise engaged and can't entertain her. But you do need her to be relatively quiet and stay nearby. You may be on the phone or trying to finish up an important project. Perhaps you are out doing errands and someone stops you to chat, or you are filling out paperwork at the bank or the post office. Here are some ideas for keeping your child entertained while you are taking care of business.

Phone Fun

When you are on the phone (thank goodness for the cordless variety) and your child is demanding your attention, here are some ways to redirect him:

- Give her a magnet and tell her to find all the things it will stick to.

- Give your child an old magazine or phone book and let him tear out the pages.

- Ask her to tie your shoes for you and then, because it will end up as a big knot, ask her to untie them.

while-mom-is-busy games

- Hand her some aluminum foil or some Baggie ties and ask her to make a sculpture.

- Give her raisins, Cheerios, mini pretzels, Goldfish crackers, gummy bears, or any similarly sized snack food and have her stir them all together in a bowl for a snack that will take a while to eat.

- Hand your child a locked padlock and key. He will love trying to unlock it.

- If two kids are vying for your attention, tell them to wad pages of old newspapers into balls for a "snowball" fight.

while-mom-is-busy games

- Pull out your folding ruler or retractable tape measure—it will amuse him long enough for you to have a short conversation.

- Pull out a photo album so that she can look at pictures of herself, or pop in a home video.

- Give your child a hole punch and a newspaper and let him punch away!

TIP: Consider investing in a headset for your cordless phone that allows you to have a hands-free conversation—very useful when you need to parent two-handed or when you are in the middle of making a meal.

"Help" Around the House

Kids have a knack for knowing when their parents *must* get something done. Just when you're trying to tidy the house for company or to finish paying the bills, that's when they suddenly *need* Barbie undressed or the train set fixed. Here are some ways to temporarily distract them:

- Have him see how many pillows he can find and how high he can stack them.

- Squirt a pile of shaving cream into the sink or on the kitchen counter for her to play with.

- Give him the feather duster and ask him to dust for you.

- If you have a deck or two of old playing cards, ask her to sort them by suit or by number.

- Ask him to sort your jar of buttons from largest to smallest.

- Suggest that she do your hair for you.

- Hand her spring-type clothespins one at a time to attach to things around the room.

- Have him match socks from the clean laundry pile or separate laundry into piles for each member of the family.

while-mom-is-busy games

- Set and then hide a kitchen timer that makes a loud ticking noise. Challenge your child to find it before it rings. This is also a great game for two kids to play together.

- Find a piece of string and a box of macaroni. Show her how to string the macaroni.

- Stretch a blanket between two pieces of furniture in the family room to make a cozy fort.

- Fill the sink a quarter full of sudsy water and give your child small plastic cups and bowls to pour with. A funnel is fun, too.

Outdoor Entertainment

If you and your kids are outside when something or someone else demands your attention, here are some things you can suggest to your little ones to keep them busy and close by:

• Ask her to find a pebble that resembles the shape of a triangle, square, circle. Or ask her to find a stone that's black, brown, gray, yellow, or reddish.

- Challenge him to find the longest stick he can. The trick is, he can't take more than ten giant steps away from you. Once he's got a stick, tell him to dig for worms or draw in the dirt. Or tell him it's a magic wand. He can decide what amazing powers it has and then . . . abracadabra!

- Let him draw with his finger on a dirty car.

- Have him drag a stick through a puddle and draw on the pavement.

- Put one stone a few feet away and tell him to throw pebbles and try to hit it.

- Point out an anthill where he can watch the action.

- If you wear a hair clip with teeth, give it to him and tell him it's a pet monster that he must feed.

baby games

Ⅰt takes a lot more stamina and ingenuity to entertain a baby than an older child. For starters, there are no residual effects of a fun game. Once the last peekaboo has come and gone, the baby's smile fades and he looks at you blankly as if nothing amusing has ever transpired. So you need to have a lot of ideas up your sleeve to keep the good times rolling, not only for the sake of the baby but for all those within earshot.

In addition, babies can neither talk well, walk well, read, draw, count, nor take part in any games requiring these skills, which would include most of the games in other sections of this book. Baby games must involve all or most of the following: immediate gratification, repetition, imitation, noise, and mess.

On the plus side, parents of babies tend to be quite prepared for a number of possibilities—from the ill-timed projectile vomit to an unexpected wait. The toys that are tucked into a pocket of the diaper bag may be all the baby needs to make it through a restaurant meal or car ride. But in the event that the Bert and Ernie rattle loses its appeal, here is a list of suggestions for entertaining the baby with the various items at hand.

Oldies but Goodies for Babies

When you are thinking up ways to amuse your baby, don't overlook all of the traditional games. Here's a refresher course:

Peekaboo

Put your hands over your face for a minute and then show your face and say, "Peekaboo! I see you!" Change your facial expression each time. Every once in a while, tease the baby by showing just part of your face.

This Little Piggy Went to Market

Beginning with
the baby's big toe,
squeeze a toe with
each line:

This little piggy went to market,
This little piggy stayed home,
This little piggy had roast beef,
This little piggy had none,
And *this* little piggy cried,
   "Wee wee wee"
All the way home!

* * * * * * * * * * * *

Itsy Bitsy Spider

Help the baby imitate a climbing
spider with her fingers:

The itsy bitsy spider
Went up the water spout.

Down came the rain,
And washed the spider out.
Out came the sun,
And dried up all the rain.
And the itsy bitsy spider
Went up the spout again!

★ ★ ★ ★ ★ ★ ★ ★ ★ ★ ★ ★

Pat-a-Cake

Clap your hands, then clap the
baby's as you say:

Pat-a-cake,
Pat-a-cake,
Baker's man,
Bake me a cake
As fast as you can.
Pat it and prick it
And mark it with B
And put it in the oven
For baby and me.

Pitty Patty Polt

Tap the bottom of the baby's feet
while you repeat this rhyme:

Pitty Patty Polt,
Shoe the wild colt!
Here a nail,
And there a nail,
Pitty Patty Polt!

★ ★ ★ ★ ★ ★ ★ ★ ★ ★ ★

See, Saw, Sacradown

Move the baby's legs as you say:

See, saw, sacradown.
This is the way to London town.
One foot up and the other foot
    down.
And that is the way to London
    town.

Startle Games

Sometimes fussiness develops a life of its own, and continues long after the reason for the initial fuss is gone. In these circumstances, babies can often be startled out of the crabbies. Do something to change their world—suddenly—so that curiosity overwhelms fussiness. Try one of these ideas:

- Holding the baby against you, lean forward so that the baby is leaning upside down.

- Bring her into a dark room or, if it's dim, bring her into a bright area.

- Pretend to drop the baby by loosening your grip on her for an instant before you grab her tightly again.

- Blow gently into the baby's face.

- Give him neck or belly raspberries.

- Lift the baby straight up, high over your head, so that she suddenly has a very different view of the world.

- Give him a spastic horsey ride
  by sitting baby in your lap
  and using your legs to slow
  down, then speed up. Then
  alternate legs up and down
  for a bumpier ride, and end
  by opening your legs so he
  "falls" through or extending
  your legs so he slides down.

Babies in a Restaurant

Making sure a baby or toddler stays continuously entertained in a restaurant is no simple feat. Here are some ideas for keeping the littlest diners happy.

Note: Some of these ideas are messy, but most restaurant folks would rather clean up a little after you leave than listen to your baby shriek for half an hour.

Jack-in-the-Box

Draw a face on your thumb. Then make a fist and tuck your thumb inside. Hum

"Here We Go Round the Mulberry Bush," and when you reach the appropriate point in the song, pop up your thumb!

Instant Present

Wrap up something from your purse—keys, a mini flashlight, a compact mirror—in several layers of napkins, placemats, foil for leftovers, or newspaper pages. Let your little one unwrap the layers as he guesses what's inside.

Homemade Stickers

Create your own stickers! Make a trip to the restroom for several sheets of paper towels. Help

your toddler tear them into little
pieces, wet each piece in your
glass of water, and then stick them
to anything within his reach. The
tearing part of this activity is fun
on its own!

Cracker Twins

Ask for a variety
of packages
of crackers,
which usually
come two to
a package.
Spread them out
on the high chair tray and ask your
toddler to find the pairs of
crackers.

Warped Reflections

Show the baby her reflection in a spoon, front and back. Or peek at the baby through a water glass.

Handy Face

Make a fist with your thumb on the outside. Draw a face on the side of your hand with the thumb as part of the lower lip (use lipstick to draw on the mouth). Your toddler can feed the face, give the face something to drink through a straw, or talk to the face.

Where's Baby?

Play peekaboo from behind a menu. Then try

playing reverse peekaboo: Put a napkin on the baby's head so that she can't see you. Then pretend you can't find her. Ask, "Where's _____? Where did she go?"

Boo!

Pointing at the ceiling, put a paper napkin over your index finger and squeeze it so it takes on a ghostly shape.

Draw a spooky face on the ghost's head and fly it around your toddler.

Hungry as a Wolf

If your toddler is growing fussy from hunger, tell him you are hungry too. Pretend to eat all sorts of odd things at the table: the napkin dispenser, the menu, the ketchup bottle. If he starts to giggle, ask him in mock surprise, "What's wrong?"

Play Dropsie

If you're really getting desperate, use your shoelaces to tie objects (like a spoon or your car keys) to the baby's high chair tray. She can drop things off the tray and pull them up again herself.

Make a Rattle
Ask your server to bring you a Styrofoam container used for leftovers. Your toddler can put various things inside, close it, and then shake it.

At the Wheel
Ask your toddler to take you for a drive using his (unbreakable) plate as a steering

wheel. You can ask him where you're going, how fast, and what kinds of things you are driving past on the way.

Monkey See, Monkey Do

Imitate your baby's actions and see how she responds. If she whacks the high chair tray with a spoon, you do the same thing.

Hands Down

Put your hands (palms down) on the high chair tray and help the baby put her hands on top of yours. Now slide your hands out from under hers and put them lightly on top of hers. Soon she'll learn to pull her hands from under yours and put them on top to keep the game going.

Babies in the Grocery Store

Babies have a limited amount of happy time in the supermarket. New sights and sounds will probably keep them amused in the short run, but if you're doing a super shop, you'll need some tricks up your sleeve.

Temporary Toys

At the beginning of your rounds, pick up a few things to amuse the baby: a box of Tic Tacs for her to shake, a bag of crinkly chips, or for those who don't like to stray from specific baby products, a toy from the baby food aisle.

Shoe Fun

Unbuckle or untie one of her shoes
and hand it to her so that she can
fiddle with it. (But don't lose it!)

Sparkly Water

If you are buying a case of bottled
water, sacrifice one (plastic) bottle
for her to play with: Stop in the
aisle that has school and office
supplies and find a small container
of glitter to buy. After you've taken
a swig from the water bottle to
make room, pour some
glitter into the bottle
and let her shake it
up and watch the
water sparkle.
(Anything small and
colorful added to the
water will be of interest.)

Balloon Bob

At most grocery stores, you can probably find a helium balloon that you can tie to the front of the cart. The baby can watch it bob along as you push the cart.

Which Way?

At the end of each aisle, ask baby which way to go. If she directs you down an aisle you've already covered, say, "Oh no, there's a monster down there!" and scoot to the aisle you intended to visit.

Babies in Waiting Rooms

A waiting room offers a number
of ways to keep a baby or toddler
happily busy.
Here are a
few:

TP Streamers

Take a few long
pieces of toilet
paper from the
restroom and let your
toddler run around the waiting
area with his streamers.

1, 2, 3 . . .

If your little one is beginning
to count, this is a great place to
practice. Count chairs, people

with glasses,
magazines on
the table,
pictures on the
wall . . .

Can You Find. .?

Find two of the same magazine
(often a pediatrician's waiting room
will have freebie parenting or
health magazines in multiples).
Give one to your child and flip
through the pages of your copy,
asking, "Can you find this happy
baby . . . this dog . . . this red car?"

Jump!

Stack magazines on the floor and
challenge your toddler to jump
over them: Can he jump over a
pile of five? How about ten?

Babies in the Doctor's Office

It gets harder to keep little guys happily engaged when you move from the waiting room to the doctor's office. There is some heightened anxiety (on your part as well as your child's!) as you get closer to the poking, prodding, measuring, and vaccinating. In addition, the space is small relative to the waiting room. But there are still some good options for keeping the fussies at bay:

Instant Puppets

Many pediatricians' offices have
stickers that are used as bribes
or rewards. Put some stickers on
the ends of tongue depressors
(or draw your own faces) and
perform an improvised puppet
show.

What Is It?

While your toddler closes his eyes,
outline an item on
the disposable
paper that covers
the exam table.
Based on the
outline, he has to
guess what the
object is.

Babies on an Airplane

You'll probably have a bag packed with airplane games, but when the toys you brought lose their appeal, try these activities:

Shady Actions

If you have a window seat, let the baby slide the window shade open and closed. Believe it or not, that might be good for 15 minutes of entertainment!

Where the Wind Blows

Move the air nozzle about so that the baby can feel the air on her hair, then her hands, then her feet, then not at all.

Peekaboo Redux

Take advantage of your peekaboo
options: Use the airline blanket,
another cooperative passenger,
the emergency card, the air
sickness bag (tuck something
inside, wait a minute, and then
pull the object out).

Instant Rattle

Request a bottle of water from
the flight attendant, guzzle it
down, and fill the empty bottle
with anything that will make a
rattling noise when the baby
shakes it.

Appendices

bag of tricks

As you can tell from the preceding pages of activities requiring no props, you can make fun from whatever is at hand. Many parents, however, like the idea of having a bag ready and waiting for a ride in the car, dinner in a restaurant, or a plane trip. If you want to create such a bag, here are some suggested rules for it:

1. Use the bag only at the specified place so that the kids don't tire of the toys.

2. Allow only a limited number of things to be taken out of the bag at one time to avoid losing toys and to ensure that there's always something new that can be taken out of the bag when the fussies set in.

3. Everything in the bag must be shared among the siblings.

Bag Basics

When you are filling your bag, stick to items that are inexpensive and replaceable, and try to avoid toys with lots of little pieces like LEGOS. Keep things like playing cards or crayons in resealable Baggies. Here are some specific items you may want to include:

bag of tricks

- Crayons and markers

- Pads of paper

- Mad Libs

- No-mess modeling clay or play dough

- Reusable stickers and sticker books

- Stopwatch or mini plastic hourglass

- Magnetic poetry set

- Matchbox cars

- Comic books

- Finger puppets

- Puzzle or trivia books

- Rubik's Cube or similar 3-D puzzles

- Playing cards and dice

- Inexpensive magnifying glass

- Travel games like magnetic checkers

- Action figures, farm animals, dinosaurs . . .

- Games like Etch A Sketch, Magna Doodle, and others that have no parts to lose

- Colored pipe cleaners

- String, yarn, or extra shoelaces

- Model books with pages that turn into airplanes or buildings

- Origami book and paper

- Blunt scissors

- Scotch tape

- Watercolor pencils (which can double as face paints)

- Sidewalk chalk

- Balloons

10 Fun Things to Do with the Balloons in Your Bag of Tricks

1. Blow up balloons and let them go: Whose goes the farthest?

2. Throw balloons as far as you can. Who wins?

3. Cross the room, tapping balloons with pencils.

4. Keep balloons up in the air while staying frozen in place.

5. Play basketball with balloons and a trash can.

6. Can two kids walk across the room with a balloon wedged between them?

7. The player who is it throws a balloon up in the air. How many kids can she tag before the balloon touches the ground?

8. Two kids stand back-to-back with a balloon wedged between them. Can they turn to the front—keeping the balloon between them—without using their hands?

9. Race to the other side of the room patting or kicking (but not holding) the balloon. Who is fastest?

10. Head outside and tie a balloon to everyone's ankle. Can the kids protect their own balloons while trying to stomp on (and burst) the other players' balloons?

Tailoring the Bag

You can individualize your Bag of Tricks depending on where it will be used.

For a Car Bag add:

- Items to play with at rest stops: a beach ball (which you can inflate to play with and deflate to repack), a Frisbee, and Hacky Sacks.

- A clipboard or lapboard for each child to make coloring and crafts easier.

- Glow Sticks that the kids can play with in the car after dark.

They will invent their own games and won't bother the driver by turning on the inside lights to do other activities.

For a Restaurant Bag add:

• Games that require a table to play: Pick-Up Sticks, Play-Doh, card games like Slamwich, and travel board games.

For an Airplane Bag add:

• Toys that kids can play with while they wait in the terminal (some of the following have the benefit of allowing them to expend some energy before being cramped in the plane): a jump rope, a small soft ball, marbles, jacks, balloons, and a yo-yo.

A Note on the Technology Age

While we hope our children will be entertained by our educational alphabet games and logic puzzles, that isn't always the way it happens. Sometimes little people, just like big people, want to sit back and be entertained. Then we resort to the wonderful gadgets available to us in the twenty-first century.

There are times when individual gizmos like GameBoys and portable CD and DVD players can help make a truly tedious wait (that second layover at the airport) more bearable. Ditto for the TV/VCR/DVD players that are made for cars and vans, and the laptop computers that can play DVDs or computer games, keeping kids happy for hours. One clever family sets up its camcorder to tape favorite TV shows at home, which the kids later watch on a flip-out viewing screen while traveling.

If you worry that the scenery is passing your kids by, you can set time limits on movies or games. After an hour or two, insist on taking a break from the video to try a few mind benders or embark on a visual scavenger hunt.

further ideas for long car rides

Here are some ideas to help make a long car ride bicker- and complaint-free when you have time to prepare in advance:

Presents

Kids love opening presents—who doesn't?—and many moms have found that perusing a dollar store or even secondhand store can result in many new-to-your-kids toys that you can wrap individually

to be opened at half-hour intervals.
Wrap them in patterned paper
towels in pre-
paration for the
inevitable juice
spills that
punctuate
every car trip.

Car Crafts

If you are an extremely well
organized parent, you can gather
all of the materials necessary to
make a given craft—clothespin
dolls, for example, would require
clothespins, yarn, felt, glue,
pipe cleaners, markers, and clay
(for a base)—and put each child's
supplies in his own shirt box
(which also doubles as a craft

surface). Though older kids are self-entertaining, they may still want to do a macramé project, for instance, with twine and beads you've provided.

Story Tapes

You can borrow these from the library, buy them at bookstores, rent them, or trade with friends. There are books on tape for every age, even the littlest children (these often come with the book itself so kids can look at the pictures while they listen). Some families like to select tapes that everyone will enjoy listening to. Classics, such as

Charlotte's Web, are great for parents and kids alike. If you have too extreme an age range to make that idea work, each child can listen to his own story on a portable tape player with headphones. Ask your librarian for suggestions on what to borrow.

more ideas for airplane trips

Here are some suggestions for making your airplane trip as pleasant as possible:

Choosing a Flight

It is much easier to keep kids happy on an airplane that is not packed to the gunwales with business travelers. To make it more likely that your flight won't be full, try to avoid the first flights in or out of major hubs or those regarded as busy "commuter" flights (generally late afternoon or early evening). If you are flying a less-full flight, ask when checking in if empty seats next to you can be blocked out to give you more room.

Direct flights seem to work out best for most families. If a layover is necessary, however, waiting in a kid-friendly airport can make the time pass quickly and enjoyably. Chicago's O'Hare Airport, for example, has a great play area suited to four- to ten-year-olds.

TIP: Don't forget to provide chewing gum for takeoff and landing! Children who are not old enough to chew gum can drink from a bottle or sippy cup or chew gummy bears.

Seating

Where you sit on a plane can determine whether or not your kids have an enjoyable flight or a miserable one. Check out www.seatguru.com for seat maps of most major airlines. This site notes which seats have the most leg room and the best view of the movie. (Avoid exit rows for the kids, and remember: You don't want a bulkhead seat because the kids' backpacks full of nifty toys will have to be stored in the overhead bin. In general, window seats are the best for kids unless you have a frequent bathroom visitor.)

airplane trips

Some parents find that taking
turns entertaining the kids on
an airplane works well. These
families seat the children with one
parent and seat the other parent
far away. The
parents can
rotate between
the "entertain
the kids" seat
and the "relax
and refresh" seat.

TIP: As you board
the plane, grab pillows
and blankets for the
kids. They are harder
to come by as the flight
progresses and people
settle in for naps.

Eat, Drink, and Keep 'Em Happy

Eating and drinking are part of
what keeps kids busy and cheerful
on planes. To make sure things go
smoothly, pack your own snacks

and drinks (especially
water) to be sure that
kids have access to

things they like. (Check out Play
with Your Food on page 333.) You
may want to call the airline ahead
of time and order kiddie meals, or
you may want to order a variety of
"special" meals so that the
kids have a
greater
choice of
food items
and can trade.
A bonus to
ordering
special meals:
You are usually
served first.

TIP: Here's a neat
way to combine a snack
with a craft activity.
Give each child a piece
of string licorice and
a Baggie of Cheerios,
Fruit Loops, or any
other cereal that has
a hole in it. The kids
can string the cereal
onto the licorice to
make necklaces and
bracelets and then
munch away when
they get hungry!

bicker busters

Sometimes no matter how hard you try to keep your kids amused, they decide to pick on one another. Trying to sort it all out is usually futile—it's best just to distract them. Here are some good ideas:

• Ask an outrageous question like, "What would you do if a huge gorilla came into the room right now and sat on that chair?"

- Do something silly like balancing a quarter on your nose. When they look intrigued, ask them to try.

- Tell them they can argue, but only in pig latin.

- Have the bickerers sit and lean backwards so that they are looking at you upside down. Now draw a face on each chin, using the upside-down mouth and adding a nose and eyes on each child's chin. See how long they can last arguing like that!

- Make them sit together on the same chair until they've made up.

- Tell them that they must sing their arguments to each other.

- If you're in a place where you can take your shoes and socks off (such as a doctor's office), draw faces on the bottoms of your kids' toes and let the toe people argue with each other.

- Have the kids sit on the floor back-to-back with their legs out and their arms linked at the elbows. Now instruct them to try to stand—keeping their arms linked and without using their hands. Cooperation will be necessary!

play with your food

5 Games to Make Snack Time More Fun

There's nothing like a little snack to make the time pass pleasantly. You can extend snack time and make it even more fun by playing one of the following snack games:

1. Cracker Puzzles: Break a handful of crackers in half and tell the kids they have to match the pieces like a puzzle.

2. Flipping Out: Flip a coin to determine how many Goldfish (or other small snacks) the kids will eat. The one who gets heads can eat five, the one who gets tails—only one.

play with your food

3. Leaning Tower of Cheerios:
See how high he can stack his Cheerios. (Hint: If he licks them first, they'll stick—and stack—better.)

4. Guess My Number:
The child who can guess the number you are thinking of (between one and ten) may eat that number of crackers, raisins, or whatever snack foods you've packed.

5. Making Faces:
See if the kids can use their snack items to create a face.

TIP: For snacks-on-the-go, avoid the inevitable spilling and bickering that come with communal snacks and pack individual ones. (This also lets you pack for particular tastes and ages.)

while you wait

Things for Moms or Dads to Do While They Wait for Their Kids

Kids aren't the only ones who wait! Parents spend countless hours waiting while kids finish up with piano lessons, swim practice, and play rehearsal. Busy parents probably have plenty of things they want to do during these waits, but in case you're in a waiting rut, here are some ideas:

1. Write a letter or card to an old friend or relative.

2. Meditate.

3. Compose a limerick or a haiku for your child or your spouse.

4. Balance your checkbook.

5. Listen to a new radio station.

6. Read a "guilty pleasure" book—not the one for your book club but something entertaining and fun.

7. Reorganize the back of the car.

8. Buy and read a magazine you've never looked at before.

9. Write out your to-do list for the day, week, and month.

10. Knit or crochet while you listen to NPR.

11. Organize the glove compartment and/or your tapes or CDs.

12. Organize your coupons and weed out the expired ones.

13. Make a mental list of the day's happiest moments.

14. Refold your maps.

15. Write out a grocery list or plan the week's menus.

16. Recline in your seat and take a power nap.

17. Formulate a five-year plan.

18. Make a holiday card list or a guest list for your next party.

19. Take a short, brisk walk or do some stretches.

20. Clean out your purse.

21. Think of all the wonderful qualities of the child you are waiting for so that when she finally emerges from her lesson/practice/rehearsal, you are genuinely delighted to see her—and she can tell.